WELSH RAILWAYS:
A Photographer's View

At Newport High Street station No. 5962 *Wantage Hall* departs into the afternoon sun for Cardiff. 23 March 1963

WELSH RAILWAYS:
A Photographer's View

Denis Dunstone

introduces

Alan Jarvis

First impression – 2002

ISBN 1 84323 153 0

© Alan Jarvis & Denis Dunstone

Alan Jarvis & Denis Dunstone have asserted their right under the Copyright, Designs and Patents Act, 1988, to be identified as Authors of this Work.

Printed in Wales at
Gomer Press, Llandysul, Ceredigion

CONTENTS

FOREWORD

One of the phenomena associated with railways in the twentieth century was the growth of railway photography. Amateurs and professionals alike found rich opportunities in the frequent steam train appearances on nearly every line – an activity which rose to a crescendo as the demise of steam became apparent. Particularly in the second half of the century the quality of photographic processing advanced and Alan Jarvis was born at a time when he was able both to enjoy the photographic possibilities and take advantage of the improving technology. Consequently, his work is highly regarded and sought-after whenever images of quality are required.

Alan's first railway pictures were taken in 1948 and, in common with others who pursued the hobby at the time, he was restricted initially to black-and-white film and fairly basic equipment. The increasing availability during the 1950s of 35 mm colour slide film, with its new process-paid facility, proved to be an important advance. As emulsions improved, so did cameras and lenses and a process of up-grading has continued over the years. Digital cameras for amateur use became available in the mid-1990s and Alan now uses both digital and film cameras. Furthermore, details of his large collection of negatives and colour slides are now held on a computer. Recently, Alan has been digitising and printing some of his early black-and-white negatives. Darkroom work was frequently regarded by many as infinitely less exciting than the actual taking of photographs and – particularly during the transitional period when the use of black-and-white film was superseded by colour – often only the best black-and-white negatives made it to the print page. The majority were stored and never printed. Now, by using the latest technology, they have a new lease of life and yield fascinating half-forgotten images of the past.

Alan's meticulous photographic technique and natural ability to compose a picture have resulted in the creation of a treasure-trove of rail scenes covering many parts of the world. The reader will derive great pleasure from careful study of the images which follow; they contain a wealth of historical, social and engineering detail impeccably recorded.

Gwyn Briwnant Jones
Cardiff, 2002

INTRODUCTION

Alan Jarvis was born in Cardiff in 1931 and has lived there ever since. He started photographing railways and tramways in 1948 and now has a collection of some 16,000 black-and-white negatives and colour slides, covering these operations in the British Isles, most of western and the former eastern Europe, Scandinavia and South Africa. His first trip abroad took place in 1959 when, during a motor-cycle tour of south-east England, he made a day trip from Folkestone to Boulogne, attracted by the return fare of 17/6d (87p, about £12 at today's values). He has crossed the English Channel by sea, air or tunnel nearly every year since.

The British railways component of his negative and slide collection contains about 6,000 photographs, 60% of which are Welsh subjects. Many have already appeared in various books and periodicals. Those which have been selected for this book cover the last years of steam trains in south and mid-Wales and very few of them have previously been published.

Concentration on the work of one photographer gives us the opportunity to re-live some of the pleasure that was to be had from the pursuit of interesting images of the railway in the days of steam. It also enables us to see the range and variety of subjects which appealed to one man. From the selection here, which represents less than 10% of his total collection of images of Wales, it will be possible to share some of Alan Jarvis's enthusiasm, not only for the steam engine, but also for the whole paraphernalia of the railway from signal-posts to architraves, from carriages to track.

Many kick themselves for not taking photographs of the steam railway when the images were out there every day but, along with others and with the help of his motor cycles, Alan has been spared this frustration, and he has made a record in depth of the railway, especially in his native Glamorgan. His particular interests and his residence in Cardiff have strongly influenced the sights he recorded and have permitted the book to fall naturally into groups of topics. So rather than being a tour at random, this book moves from one subject to another. This concentration on topics enables locations and activities to be examined from different angles and in varying light and helps those less familiar with the scene to gain a feel for the setting.

Residence close to the busy railway world around Cardiff enabled Alan to capture the scene in weather conditions which themselves, in many instances, enhanced the image. He has a particular liking for the soft late afternoon light of winter and some of his most appealing images reflect this. But he also has an eye for the unusual, and frequently finds unexpected interest in what might at first sight seem of no importance. He also enjoys the Welsh landscape and derives satisfaction from recording the way the railway engineers coped with the hills, rivers and valleys.

The groups of photographs which follow relate, in the main, to particular geographical areas. Each area is introduced with a brief historial sketch and physical description which, together with maps where appropriate, is intended to make easier the understanding of the location of the photographs. Interspersed with the photographs are Alan's personal recollections and anecdotes. But first he recalls how he started, his apparatus, and his means of transport.

HOW IT ALL STARTED

My earliest recollection of a steam train in motion is from my pram, probably in 1934 at the age of three. A bridge across the former Rhymney Railway to Caerphilly lay between our house and the local shops and my mother dreaded the journey if I was with her as I would insist on waiting for the passage of a train. Invariably one would pass just before we reached the bridge or just after we had left after a long, fruitless wait. A tearful journey home would follow.

A vivid memory is of Torquay station in 1939 returning from holiday on the day before war with Germany was declared. The platforms were packed with apprehensive home-going holiday-makers although I was too young to realise the implications. As we walked through the booking-hall a train passed through the station hauled by a red-painted locomotive. I had no more than a glimpse through the throng and at that age my knowledge of locomotive types was limited – I knew only of black or green engines. Presumably the disruption of normal traffic movements had already started.

Before and during the war one of my aunts lived in my young idea of paradise, with the GWR main line to Swansea at the bottom of the garden and the former Taff Vale Railway, Penarth to Radyr line, along the front of the house. In those days youngsters were able to walk the streets free of fear and as the house was less than a mile from my home I was allowed to spend many evenings there until darkness or bedtime arrived. Another clear memory, probably at the time of the evacuation from Dunkirk, is of an LNER locomotive passing on a westbound Red Cross ambulance train when dusk was already well advanced. The number 7749 has stuck in my head for many years but recent research has led me to believe that it was probably No. 7479, a 4-6-0 of the 'B12' Class.

Towards the end of the war short trips were made to such places as Newport and Bristol. Newport provided my first close contact with an LMS engine on the passenger service from Tredegar. I stared at the totally unfamiliar five-figure number 27663 which to me, accustomed to neat GWR number plates, appeared enormous in size as well as numerically.

I was invited into the cab of this Webb 0-6-2 'Coal Tank' and was immediately struck by the strange, almost fishy, smell which was totally different from that of GWR locomotives. I later realised that this was probably related to the type of coal.

At Bristol there was the hope of seeing at least one GWR 'King'. These locomotives were banned from south Wales due to their 22½ ton axle loading. I eventually saw one but the enduring memory is of seeing GWR 'Castle' Class No. 5069 and LMS 'Jubilee' No. 5572 at adjacent platforms and thinking how much superior was the vast and gleaming GWR arc proclaiming

compared with the minuscule LMSR nameplate

E I R E

There were two quite special trains I remember during my early 'teens. In the light evenings I was permitted to delay my homework until I had been to a nearby vantage point to see the 'up' milk and fish trains. The fish usually preceded the milk by about 15 minutes at around 6.50pm. Apart from the overpowering and lingering smell from the well-used crates there was little of note about the fish train – it was usually powered by a local 'Hall' or 'Grange' Class locomotive and ran from Milford Haven to the London area. But the milk train, from Whitland to Kensington, invariably produced a 'Castle' and very often a rare one, perhaps not seen before, maybe from Wolverhampton or Plymouth. It would have worked 'down' in the morning and presumably Old Oak Common depot in London used whatever was to hand. The milk tanks were heavy three-axle vehicles and produced a distinctive three-beats-to-the-bar rhythm passing over the joints in the 60 ft rails, rounded off by the two beats from the vacuum-braked guard's van. Then back to algebra, history, French, etc.

GETTING ABOUT

My mobility increased with the acquisition of a pedal cycle when full production was resumed in 1945 and was greatly enhanced when I became mechanically propelled in 1953. This was first achieved by the conversion of my pedal cycle into a moped by the addition of a 49cc bolt-on petrol engine. From there I rose through 197cc, 250cc, 350cc and 650cc machines, ending my motor-cycling days in 1973 when I rather sorrowfully parted with a Triumph 650cc twin in favour of a belt-driven DAF car. But for train chasing, there was nothing to beat a high-powered motor cycle with its rapid acceleration and manoeuvrability through traffic.

Although this collection of photographs is confined to Wales, I also covered a lot of southern and western England. The GWR and BR(WR) provided a dedicated service for the conveyance of motor cars and motor cycles with sidecars through the Severn tunnel between Severn Tunnel Junction and Pilning stations, with vehicles being securely chained down and chocked on flat wagons. A tarpaulin cover was available at extra cost. This service was started in 1924 and although much more reliable than the tide- and weather-dependent Beachley to Aust river ferry, dating from 1926, and considerably less hair-raising, with no slippery, right-angled loading ramps, it never seemed to attract much patronage and I knew several car owners who had no knowledge of the tunnel facilities. This service was also available to solo motor cyclists, who could stow their machines in the brake/third carriage used to convey the car drivers and their passengers. But any passenger train which was booked to stop at both stations was available to solo motor cycle riders and I used this service a great deal, often with a friend on the pillion. The single fare through the tunnel was 3s 11d (20p) for my motor cycle and 1s 1d (5p) for me. There were portable loading ramps on each platform and many summer Saturdays or weekdays off work would find me sitting on my machine parked on the platform at Severn Tunnel Junction with the ramp at the ready waiting for the 9.15am train. Then the exertion of pushing a heavy motor cycle up into the luggage compartment, sometimes, but not always, with the help of the guard (some would attend merely to close the double doors and would stand watching me struggling). On one occasion I felt a strong shove from the rear and found the pusher to be the engine driver, a model engineering friend of mine. A memorable trip through the tunnel on the footplate of a GWR 'Grange' followed. I discovered that I was not popular with weekday commuters, as the loading of my motor cycle, especially if I was at the wrong end of the platform for the van, added minutes to their journeys to work or home. I use the singular, as very rarely were there any other motor cyclists waiting with me. On just a few occasions, after a long ride in the rain from a sortie into the West Country, I accepted defeat at Pilning and stayed on the train with my motor cycle all the way to Cardiff.

This service ended with the opening of the M4 and the first Severn road bridge. When a bigger and better road bridge was proposed – the so-called Second Severn Crossing (SSC) – the pre-eminence of roads over railways, at least in the mind of officialdom, became apparent. Disregarding several ferries, which plied across the narrower section of the river Severn above Aust over a period of several centuries, the SSC was pre-dated by the Aust Ferry, the New Passage Ferry, the railway tunnel and the railway bridge between Lydney and Sharpness, as well as the first M4 road bridge. That makes the second road bridge the Sixth Severn Crossing, still the SSC as it happens!

CAMERAS

Apart from a pre-war Kodak Brownie box camera loaned to me by my parents, my first camera was a folding Kershaw Curlew using 120 roll-film, size 3½" x 2½", allowing 8 exposures per roll which I developed and printed myself. This camera was purchased in late 1952 on my release from National Service. All the monochrome pictures in this book were taken with this camera which served me well until 1959 when, having been impressed by my friends' results with 35mm colour slides, I changed to this medium.

My first camera for colour photography was an Ilford Advocate, finished in white enamel. Its reasonable price attracted me and it turned out to be quite a good buy with a lens capable of very crisp results, although the maximum shutter speed was only 1/125 sec. But I had not taken sufficient care to study the full specification – it was fitted with quite a wide-angle lens of 35mm focal length. This meant that I had to stand quite near the subject to ensure a reasonably well-filled frame. As a result I was continually being 'oyed' at by other photographers with more normal 45 or 50mm lenses as I was intruding into their viewfinders.

Two years later I bought an Agfa Silette with a more conventional lens and the yelling ceased. At about the same time the speed of Kodachrome jumped to an amazing 25 ASA which gave a much better chance of success in poor lighting conditions, as well as allowing a higher shutter speed for fast-moving trains.

In 1968 the Silette was traded in for my first single-lens reflex camera, a Praktica, and other makes followed. However, I have retained the Advocate for sentimental reasons. Most of the photographs in this book were taken with Kodak slide film although a few are on Agfacolor. In common with some of my contemporaries I tried other makes of film in search of cheapness or higher emulsion speed. The penalty tended to be a more grainy picture. Most of the resulting slides have since degraded into various shades of pink or green. It has been possible to recover some of them by copying with colour filtration but, in the main, they are lost for historical purposes, certainly as colour records.

After the end of main line steam in south Wales I made more frequent visits to areas where it still had some time left, as did many of my friends. Industrial locomotive photography was also given more attention. I did not, however, indulge in the popular trek up to Scotland to view the LNER A4 Pacifics having their final fling. Northern France was only a little over half the distance from Cardiff and visits to that area were eventually extended to most of Europe and Scandinavia, including the former Iron Curtain countries where the fact that railway photography was regarded as a subversive activity added spice to the proceedings: 'You may take a photograph of the locomotive but not the building behind it nor the bridge it is standing on. The guards are armed.' It is disturbing to note that railway photography is now being discouraged on some main line UK stations apparently for reasons of 'commercial confidentiality'.

Chapter 1

THE GWR MAIN LINE IN SOUTH WALES

The former South Wales Railway built the line from Chepstow to Carmarthen and New Milford (as Neyland was first called). Completion of the bridge over the Wye at Chepstow in 1852 enabled the first link to be made between south Wales and London by way of Gloucester. Subsequently, in 1886, the Severn tunnel was opened, though until 1906 London trains had to travel by way of Bristol. The following selection visits the eastern and western extremities of southern Wales and some intermediate locations. St Fagans is given more detailed treatment later.

Severn Tunnel West and Fishguard

The GWR main line entered Wales below ground via the Severn tunnel. In June 1962, a 'Hall' Class locomotive passes Severn Tunnel West signal-box with a train from Portsmouth. The GWR signal has the older 5 ft arms used when set more than 26 feet above rail level. The wheel inside the finial atop the post was part of the lamp winding mechanism.

No. 4079 *Clun Castle* heads an enthusiasts' special into the tunnel. 18 April 1964

'5100' Class 2-6-2T No. 5110 pilots a BR Class 9 2-10-0 on an eastbound coal train which is leaving No. 1 'up' loop for the journey through the tunnel. Two loops were necessary during the Second World War to hold trains until a path could be found through the tunnel which did not interfere with more urgent traffic. April 1960

140 miles from the Severn tunnel, pannier tank No. 9602 awaits departure from Fishguard Harbour station with a local train for Carmarthen. The cliffs visible in the background were formed by blasting away the headland for the construction of the harbour and station which were opened in 1906. 6 September 1962

NEWPORT

The complex railway pattern at Newport was caused partly by geography, but mainly by the fact that until 1872 the South Wales Railway was broad gauge whereas the gauges of the tramroads were something less. When they were converted into railways in the 1850s they became standard gauge. So, as at Cardiff and Swansea, there was no connection between the local valley railways and the south Wales main line. The Western Valley passenger trains used a small station at Dock Street and the Eastern Valley trains used a station at Mill Street. In 1874, once the broad gauge had been removed, a new line from Pontypool to the south Wales main line east of Newport rendered the station at Mill Street redundant. In 1879 direct connection was made between the main line and the Western Valleys line enabling Dock Street to be closed. This link passed from Gaer Junction on the main line just south of the platforms at Newport station through the Gaer tunnel to Park Junction.

North of Park Junction was the location of the so-called 'Golden Mile' where six parallel tracks conveyed some 4 million tons of coal a year (not forgetting the return empties) with a toll to the landowner on every one. Further north were the sidings at Rogerstone where the coal trains were deposited pending movement to the docks.

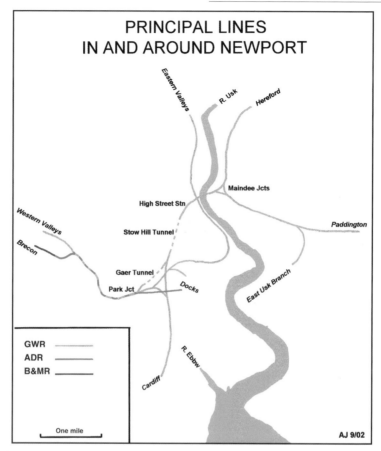

PRINCIPAL LINES
IN AND AROUND NEWPORT

Eastern Valleys

R. Usk

Hereford

Maindee Jcts

High Street Stn

Western Valleys

Stow Hill Tunnel

Paddington

Brecon

Gaer Tunnel

Docks

Park Jct

East Usk Branch

GWR
ADR
B&MR

R. Ebbw

Cardiff

One mile

AJ 9/02

Alan confesses he would probably not have taken this photograph had it not been for the presence of GWR chocolate and cream in an otherwise totally Midland-flavoured train. Type 4 diesel hydraulic No. D1051 *Western Ambassador* is less than eight months old as it enters the station with the 7.05 am from Penzance. 23 March 1963

Two GWR heavy tank locomotives pass on Newport bridge. On the left is a 2-8-0T on a train of open wagons. A 2-8-2T tank is hauling the 'down' train, which appears to consist of bogie wagons. The 2-8-0T locomotives dated back to 1910. In 1934 55 of them were rebuilt with extended coal bunkers to enable them to haul coal trains from south Wales over longer distances. March 1961.

With two brake vans sandwiched between them, 2-8-0T No. 5251 and a Type 3 diesel head westwards through the station. In earlier days the high building on platform 1 contained a well-appointed GWR restaurant with table service provided by traditionally attired waitresses. 24 April 1963

Heading west, 2-8-0 No. 2872 trundles its train of unfitted open wagons down the through line. 15 May 1963

In the early 1960s traffic flows through Newport High Street station were altered to cope with increased movements of iron ore and steel traffic from the new Llanwern steelworks. Freight and passenger trains were segregated and most 'down' passenger trains were shifted to the north-side platforms to allow clear paths for freight trains. In this view of 23 March 1963, No. 6919 *Tylney Hall* is about to leave for Cardiff with a train of mainly green-liveried Southern Region stock from Portsmouth. The train is using what was previously the main 'up' platform.

A 'Hall' Class locomotive No. 6919 *Tylney Hall* prepares to leave Newport High Street station with a train for Cardiff. 18 May 1959

On the Cardiff side of Newport station the lines penetrated Stow Hill via two parallel tunnels. A 'Castle' Class locomotive heads an 'up' express past Gaer Junction into the original (1850) tunnel from the 'up' relief line. March 1961

Looking east over Park Junction. A Class '4200' 2-8-0T, bunker-first, has climbed through Gaer tunnel, visible in the middle distance, from Gaer Junction on the main line. 23 March 1963

No. 5209 is approaching Park Junction from Newport Docks with a long train of vans. 23 March 1963

Near Marshfield Alan witnessed a narrow escape from a serious accident. In his own words Alan takes up the story, 'Due to signalling equipment deficiences at the signal-box to the rear, a light engine running tender-first had been been allowed into a section of track already occupied by a gangers' petrol-driven trolley which was engaged in minor track maintenance with frequent stops. The ganger on lookout duty saw the approaching locomotive and shouted a warning. The gang leapt aboard the trolley and drove off at all possible speed, apparently unseen by the driver of the light engine which was closing in on the trolley. The situation was saved by the action of the Marshfield signalman who threw his signal back to "danger". The trolley careered past the signal but the locomotive pulled up, the driver demanding to know why the signal had been returned to "danger" in his face.'

'Hall' Class No. 4995 *Easton Hall* heading eastwards near Marshfield with a Portsmouth train of mainly Southern Region stock. Various shades of green dominate this scene which was taken into the light from a noon sun which brings out the reflections from the surface of the well-used rails. The blossom on the hawthorn (May) bushes accords with the date of the photograph. 14 May 1963

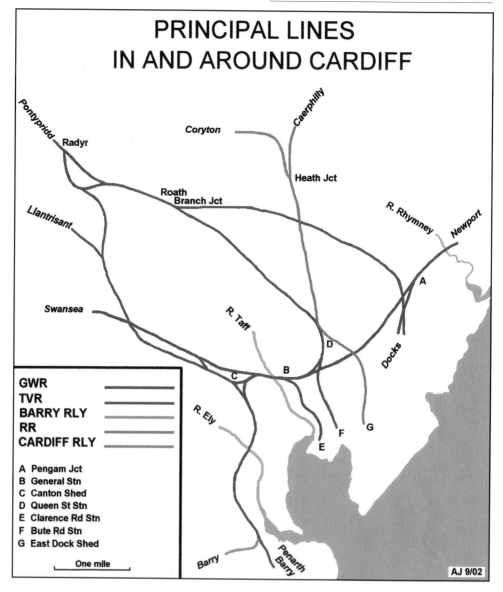

PRINCIPAL LINES
IN AND AROUND CARDIFF

GWR
TVR
BARRY RLY
RR
CARDIFF RLY

A Pengam Jct
B General Stn
C Canton Shed
D Queen St Stn
E Clarence Rd Stn
F Bute Rd Stn
G East Dock Shed

One mile

AJ 9/02

CARDIFF

For centuries no more than a small town with a castle and parish church on the east
bank of the Taff river, Cardiff began to grow at the end of the eighteenth century
when a port was needed to ship minerals from the Merthyr Tydfil area. Then and
until later in the nineteenth century, Merthyr was the largest town in Wales and the
largest centre of iron manufacture in the world. Cardiff was at the mouth of the Taff
which, although itself not navigable, had carved a long picturesque valley from the
Brecon Beacons to the Bristol Channel. Just north of Cardiff at Taff's Well this
valley becomes narrow and steeply wooded as it breaks through the last line of
hills, which themselves seem to act as a protective barrier against the north.

Down the valley was laid first the Glamorgan canal and then, in 1841, the Taff Vale Railway. This was a standard gauge mainly mineral line and therefore had no physical connection with the broad gauge South Wales Railway when that appeared on the scene in 1851. This was the predecessor of the Great Western and, having as its objective a fast route to Ireland by way of Fishguard, passed through Cardiff on its way west without, as it were, looking to either right or left. The initial focus of its interest was passenger traffic rather than freight. Until the broad gauge was reduced to standard along this route in 1872, no physical connection was possible between the GWR and the local valley railways.

Next on the scene was the Rhymney Railway which crossed over a pass through the mountains separating the Rhymney valley from the Taff and, in 1858, joined the Taff Vale Railway main line just north of Taff's Well. In 1871 this was augmented by a direct line from the Rhymney valley to Cardiff, cut through Caerphilly Mountain.

Cardiff thrived as a port and under the influence of the landowner, the Bute family, was expanded to cope with the rising need for shipping coal. By the end of the nineteenth century it was the largest coal exporting port in the world. It therefore became necessary to diversify the access routes to the port. The city also grew as an administrative centre with a large middle-class population. This led to a need for passenger transport alongside the carriage of coal and minerals. A commuter network was developed. Penarth to the south-west became not only an extra port, but also a desirable place to live.

CARDIFF MAIN LINE EAST

A possible earlier difference of opinion appears to have been resolved as 2-6-0 No. 6328 and a 'Hall' make their way briskly out of Cardiff on the 'up' relief line. 25 May 1963

No. 6956 *Mottram Hall* gets to grips with a mixed assortment of wagons as it heads up the main line a little to the east of Rumney River Bridge Junction. The cooling towers of Roath power station were demolished in 1972. The name of the river is the Rhymney, but the nearby residential area is known as Rumney. 23 April 1963

BR Class 9 2-10-0 No. 92225 takes its load of frost-covered coal on to the Roath Dock branch at Pengam Junction on a misty morning in January 1964.

Pengam Junction, on the eastern approaches to Cardiff, was always a scene of activity. A 'County' Class 4-6-0 accelerates a Paignton train past the signal-box after a signal check. 'Hall' Class No. 6965 *Thirlestaine Hall* has started to depart from the coal yard with a long train, mainly of coke. 8 August 1963

CARDIFF GENERAL STATION

The 'Red Dragon' from Swansea has arrived at platform 2 behind an unidentified 'Hall' Class locomotive. Smartly turned out by the cleaners at Canton shed, No. 6003 *King George IV* waits in the middle road to take over for the journey to Paddington. September 1960

No. 7900 *St Peter's Hall* pulls out of platform 2 with a train bound for Plymouth. 6 April 1963.

'Castle' Class No. 5000 *Launceston Castle* stands at platform 1 awaiting departure time with the 8.52pm to Bristol. 24 February 1953.

Heading the inaugural 'up' 'Pembroke Coast Express', No. 5082 *Swordfish* is about to pull out from platform 1 on 8 June 1953. This locomotive carried the name *Powis Castle* until 1941, when it became one of twelve members of the class to receive the names of aircraft which took part in the Battle of Britain.

Later on 8 June, No. 7027 *Thornbury Castle* enters the station with the first 'down' 'Pembroke Coast Express'.

CANTON AND EAST DOCK SHEDS

Canton shed was built in 1882 by the GWR and was its largest depot in Wales, with some 120 locomotives regularly stabled there. It survives in 2002 as a diesel depot located close to the main line west of Cardiff station. For many years it had a conveniently placed footbridge across the whole site, much fequented by photographers. Alan Jarvis records that for several years in the 1950s he visited Canton every day as it was host to a wide variety of GWR locomotives, both passenger and freight.

East Dock shed was opened in 1931 on the site of a former Rhymney Railway shed known as Cardiff Docks. It was built by the GWR with funds made available by the government to encourage an improvement in infrastructure and to provide work. It housed some 70 locomotives. It was first closed to steam engines in 1958 when it became a base for diesel shunters. However, it enjoyed a revival in 1962 when Canton was closed to steam engines which were shifted to East Dock until final closure in 1965. Its prime function was as a base for locomotives engaged in freight work on the valley lines and in the docks.

In Alan's words, 'Canton was, and still is, the foregathering point for enthusiasts from far and wide. To this day I occasionally look in, some 55 years after my first visit. The great attraction has always been its easy visibility from a footbridge in De Croche Place, off Ninian Park Road. Until the premises were converted to a diesel depot the footbridge, which now only crosses the main lines, extended across the full width of the shed and yard and the unwritten rule has always been that enthusiasts are tolerated as long as they remain on the footbridge. In the last few years of its existence as a steam depot a few privileged folk were given the run of the place on the understanding that they behaved responsibly. A Christmas Day morning visit was *de rigeur* and it was not unknown for us to be summoned into the foreman's office for seasonal hospitality.'

Wolverhampton-built pannier tank Class '2021' No. 2147 of 1904 stands in the yard at the rear of the shed. Unlike many members of the class this locomotive retained its open cab until scrapped in March 1953. 25 December 1952

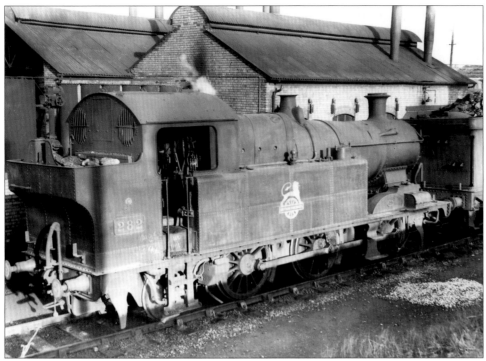

On Christmas Day 1952 No. 282 an ex-TVR Class 04 0-6-2T awaits its turn in the ash disposal/coaling queue. In those days work continued throughout the Christmas period.

'Saint' Class 4-6-0 No. 2920 *Saint David* has been coaled and awaits its next turn of duty on 25 April 1953. In 1952, when travelling back to barracks at Farnborough, Alan timed this locomotive hauling his 12-coach London train at 92 mph near Uffington. This was done by counting the number of rail joints in 41 seconds, this number being equal to the speed in mph. Alan regrets the replacement of standard 60 feet lengths of rail by long welded sections which put a stop to this entertaining pastime. Unlike timing mileposts with a stop-watch, it could be practised after dark and in tunnels and gave equally accurate results.

A view of Canton showing the well-known footbridge and a varied selection of motive power including ex-Alexandra Docks 2-6-2T No. 1205 in the foreground. 18 July 1953

The fireman seems oblivious to the incomplete combustion of the coal with which he has just fed the fire of 2-8-0 locomotive No. 2876. According to Alan this was an uncharacteristic display at Canton. March 1961

Engines repaired at Caerphilly works usually paid a visit to Canton on their way back to their home shed. Collett 0-6-0 No. 2241 gleams in the sun of an April day in 1961.

The class that got away. Sadly no representative of the 'Grange' Class survived into preservation. They were versatile locomotives and very popular with enginemen. No. 6822 *Manton Grange* carries the name of a stately home near Marlborough in Wiltshire. The white patches on the boiler are notices warning firemen of the danger of overhead live wires when manipulating the long fire-irons stowed along the side of the tender. 16 July 1962

Two 'Halls' and a 'Castle' are ready for duty at the front of the shed. The footbridge which spanned the full width of the shed frames the picture. 24 July 1962.

In the last few months of its existence as a steam shed, Canton hosted more 'foreign' locomotives than ever before. LMS 'Jubilees' became fairly regular visitors and on at least one occasion an LMS 'Crab' 2-6-0 arrived after working a freight from Saltley, Birmingham. One of these, No. 42784 is ready to leave for its Midlands home. The nickname was derived from the scuttling appearance given by the prominent valve gear. 15 August 1962

Two 'Grange' Class locomotives, Nos. 6853 *Moorhampton Grange* and 6860 *Aberporth Grange* stand in shafts of sunlight in an otherwise empty shed on the last day of its life as a steam depot. 9 September 1962.

CARDIFF EAST DOCK SHED

No. 92 was an ex-Rhymney Railway Class S1 0-6-0T. It was one of a class of three delivered to the Rhymney Railway only three years before the absorption of the company into the GWR in 1923. After absorption, most locomotives of the pre-grouping south Wales railway companies were rebuilt with standard GWR boilers but a number retained their original boilers until scrapped. No. 92 was one of them and was withdrawn in June 1964. 26 December 1952

After this shed's reincarnation as a main line servicing facility following the closure of Canton, 'Castle' Class No. 5056 *Earl of Powis* stands on the track that served both for ash removal and coaling. 28 July 1963

One of the dirtiest jobs of steam locomotive maintenance, cleaning out the accumulated ashes from the smokebox, is being performed on an LMS-designed Class 8F 2-8-0. 29 March 1963

In the final few years Alan managed to photograph main line engines of each of the former 'Big Four' companies and British Railways at Cardiff East Dock shed. Southern Railway Maunsell-designed 2-6-0 Class U No. 31613, withdrawn in January 1964, is in steam but is destined for Bird's scrapyard at Morriston, along with seven of its also doomed comrades which it had hauled from the Southern Region. It stands next to GWR 'County' Class 4-6-0 No. 1010 *County of Caernarvon*. Built in 1945 this locomotive was named *County of Carnarvon* in December 1947. The spelling was corrected in November 1951. It was withdrawn in the month that the photograph was taken. 2 July 1964

LMS-designed but LNER-built, Class 8F 2-8-0 No. 48503 stands at the coaling stage. A shiny black locomotive is not always a good photographic subject but, in this case, the angle of the sun serves to provide some contrast. 5 June 1965

A pannier tank inside the shed confronts an alien in the form of LNER Class K1 2-6-0 No. 62057. Allocated to York, this most unusual visitor had arrived after working a freight train from Washwood Heath, Birmingham, to Stoke Gifford, Bristol. Also present this day were a number of ex-LMS Class 5 and 8F locomotives from sheds whose motive power did not normally reach south Wales, for example Stockport, Stoke-on-Trent, Rugby and Nottingham. The reason for these unusual workings was the disruption in the supply of coal caused by a coal miners' strike. 5 June 1965

Two of the Riddles-designed BR Class 9F 2-10-0s and a Stanier Class 8F 2-8-0 stand silhouetted in the doorways of the shed. July 1965

CARDIFF MAIN LINE WEST

Viewed from the celebrated footbridge at Canton locomotive shed, 0-6-0 PT No. 9752 saunters along the 'up' main line while 'Castle' Class No. 5092 *Tresco Abbey* reverses towards a train of empty milk tanks which it will be taking to Whitland. 1 October 1962

On an unusually sunny day in the harsh January of 1963 No. 6942 *Eshton Hall* heads a vacuum-fitted freight train past Canton locomotive shed. The wooden scaffolding will eventually carry a notice announcing the conversion of the premises to a diesel maintenance depot. Most of the GWR express locomotives were named after stately homes in the area served by the railway but there were exceptions. Eshton Hall is near Skipton in north Yorkshire.

A pleasing scene in the late afternoon sun of Boxing Day 1961. A 'Castle' passes Leckwith Junction with a Paddington to Swansea express. The 'down' goods running loop is still active today and is sometimes used by passenger trains to allow them to overtake freight trains on the main line.

The spring of 1963 has at last arrived. On 22 April, 'Castle' Class No. 5043 *Earl of Mount Edgcumbe* is hauling a Bristol to Swansea train past the still empty scaffolding.

A '7200' Class 2-8-2T No. 7250 entering Ely (Main Line) station in the western suburbs of Cardiff with an 'up' loose-coupled freight train. The old carriage on the platform was in use as a classroom for the Mutual Improvement Association. Ely had the unusual sub-title 'Main Line' presumably to avoid confusion with the eponymous cathedral city in East Anglia. September 1959

The snow had disappeared by the time this photograph was taken in afternoon sunshine on 23 March 1963. Ex-LMS 8F No. 48707 has passed out of the Plymouth Woods and is approaching Ely (Main Line) station with an 'up' van train.

At the same location as the preceding photograph, but in more verdant conditions on 27 July 1962, steam merges with the clouds as 2-8-0T No. 4267 heads a coal train towards Cardiff.

ST FAGANS

Some four miles west of Cardiff, the GWR main line to Swansea and Carmarthen was crossed by the Barry Railway main line heading north from Barry to the Rhondda and Rhymney valleys. A spur linked the two lines from north to east. Its descent was made sufficiently gradual by taking the line in an extended curve beneath the overbridge. It was a favoured location for photography with an old and attractive station, plenty of action, and a fine viaduct for background.

Class '2800' No. 3827 sounded as run-down as it looked as it endeavoured to hurry through St Fagans station with a 'down' train of vacuum-braked wagons. 4 June 1962

'Hall' Class No. 4966 *Shakenhurst Hall* passes St Fagans station on 12 January 1963 with a 'down' freight train. Snow had started to fall on 26 December 1962 and it lingered until well into March 1963.

Looking west from St Fagans station the auto-train 'JB' can be seen approaching along the Barry Railway branch from Tyn-y-Caeau Junction. The signalman appears to have his hands on the large 'ship's wheel' ready to open the level crossing gates to road traffic when the train has passed. The highest signal on the gantry controlled the 'down' main line and the left-hand arm the 'down' running loop. The right-hand arm cleared entry on to the branch. The function of the missing arm would have been to indicate entry on to the branch and then left into the former GWR/Barry Railway exchange sidings. 1954

A pannier tank heads westwards from St Fagans with a train of steel wagons. Ahead of the locomotive an arch of the Barry Railway viaduct can be glimpsed. The unusual signal, with holes in the arm, controlled the reversing of trains from the 'down' main into the running loop which commenced at St Fagans signal-box and would normally have been a ground signal. 12 April 1963

A Class '4200' 2-8-0T heads a train of coal wagons in the direction of St Fagans. At this time it was the practice to paint vacuum-braked wagons in red oxide to distinguish them from unfitted wagons, which were grey. 12 April 1963

There were several places in south Wales where members of the Royal Family could spend the night on board their train. The locations were quiet and secluded. The branch to the Severn Tunnel pumping station was one, and Wenvoe station goods yard was another. Alan records: 'I received curious, probably suspicious, stares from the footplate inspector and accompanying Guardians of Royalty when I took photographs of this, the empty Royal Train train at four different points. Its route and timings were certainly not made available to the public at large but could be deduced from local knowledge. In this photograph, taken in September 1961, the train has come off the GWR main line at St Fagans and is now on the chord line leading up to the Barry main line with the locomotive, an ex-GWR 2-6-0, running tender-first. At Tyn-y-caeau Junction it will reverse direction, the locomotive running around the train and proceed down the Barry main line in the evening light to Wenvoe where the visiting Royal party will join it for the night.

'A signalman who had worked at Wenvoe signal-box related to me how, early one morning, a workmen's train was coming down the Barry main line from Pontypridd. The occupied Royal Train was snug in its siding at Wenvoe but the driver of the workmen's train hadn't read his weekly notices properly or had forgotten it would be there. Emerging from Wenvoe tunnel at about 5.30am he spotted various people strolling around the sidings and running lines at Wenvoe in the dawn light. He did what he should have done had the circumstances been normal – he grabbed the whistle chord and hung on to it all the way through Wenvoe station and beyond. I cannot say whether he was beheaded or simply reprimanded.

'On another occasion, again at Wenvoe, the fireman of a passing train hurled out several large lumps of coal to feed the signalman's stove – a common practice almost everywhere. One lump pierced a lineside electrical equipment cabinet and locked up all the signalling just before the Royal Train was about to depart.'

In Alan's experience it was rare for this situation to arise with such precision in the presence of a photographer. To the west of St Fagans in 1954 an 'up' express hauled by No. 7028 *Cadbury Castle* passes a freight train in the hands of No. 90693, an 'Austerity' 2-8-0. Designed by R.A. Riddles, 935 of these locomotives were built by North British and Vulcan between 1943 and 1945. They were used by the War Department and all four main line companies. As the liberation of Europe advanced, many of them were sent to France, Belgium and Holland. Some found their way to Sweden and China. 150 similar engines were built at around the same time with the 2-10-0 wheel arrangement.

'Grange' Class No. 6812 *Chesford Grange* is about to pass under the Barry Railway viaduct with the 3.25pm Cardiff to Swansea stopping train. 26 August 1953

'Castle' Class No. 4081 *Warwick Castle* takes the 8.55am Paddington to Pembroke Dock (the 12.15pm departure from Cardiff) underneath the Barry Railway viaduct near St Fagans. 23 March 1953

Shortly afterwards '4200' Class 2-8-0T No. 5218 passes with a loose-coupled freight, having been held in the goods loop at St Fagans to allow *Warwick Castle* to overtake.

West of St Fagans, 'Mogul' No. 6373 approaches the arches of the Barry Railway viaduct with an 'up' stopping train from Porthcawl. 4 August 1962

The fireman of 2-8-2T No. 7246 takes a breath of air as his train of concrete sleepers rolls west near the hamlet of St George's. 18 August 1962.

SWANSEA

Like Cardiff, Swansea lies at the mouth of a river which is itself not navigable. But whereas Cardiff was to grow in the nineteenth century as a port and administrative centre, Swansea had been a centre of industry since as early as the thirteenth century. The source of its success was readily accessible coal lying near the surface. On this a minerals manufacturing business was founded which lasts in truncated form to the present-day. During the nineteenth and the early part of the twentieth century, Swansea was a world leader in the manufacture of copper, then tin-plate, zinc and nickel. In addition, anthracite was discovered in the hills to the north-west and coal in the upper Tawe valley. As a result, Swansea became a significant coal exporter.

The railway layout was complex, due mainly to the geography, but also due to the first line of the South Wales Railway crossing to the north of the city and making it necessary that the main station in the centre be built at the end of a branch. Efforts to overcome this failed. As a result, Swansea at the height of the railway age had six passenger terminal stations. For many years, GWR trains on the main line stopped only at Landore, where it was necessary to change for Swansea. The Midland had a terminus on the east side of the river, and the LNWR line from Shrewsbury approached the city along the coast from the west, parallel to the Mumbles Railway. The Rhondda & Swansea Bay had a small station in the eastern dock area as did the GWR for its low level line from Neath. The final development came in 1913 when the GWR completed a by-pass from east of Llanelli to west of Neath called the Swansea District Line. This passed north of the south Wales main line and besides shortening the route from Fishguard to London, eased the gradients for freight trains.

No. 3693 stands out of use in the yard at Swansea East Dock shed. March 1961

No. 5054 *Earl of Ducie*, emitting contrasting smoke and steam at Swansea High Street station, is awaiting departure with the 'up' 'Pembroke Coast Express'. No. 9762 is on station pilot duty and an engine driver's lunch awaits collection. 26 April 1963

The rightful owner of the lunch is revealed as No. 5054 gets into its stride.

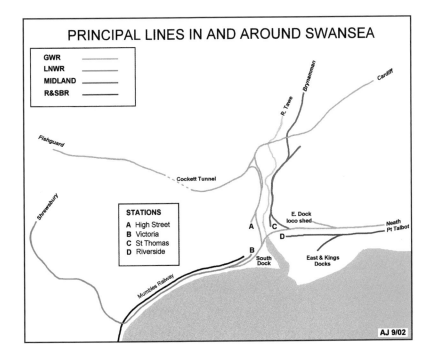

PRINCIPAL LINES IN AND AROUND SWANSEA

GWR _____
LNWR _____
MIDLAND _____
R&SBR _____

R. Tawe
Brynamman
Cardiff
Fishguard
Cockett Tunnel
Shrewsbury

STATIONS
A High Street
B Victoria
C St Thomas
D Riverside

E. Dock loco shed
A
C
D
Neath
Pt Talbot
B
South Dock
East & Kings Docks
Mumbles Railway

AJ 9/02

A BR standard 2-6-2T leaves Swansea Victoria with a local train. The driver of No. 3604 sportingly agreed to provide some matching steam for the photographer by moving his empty coaches a few yards at the same time. 26 April 1963

Chapter 2

A DAY IN THE LIFE OF AN AUTO-TRAIN – THE 'PONTYPRIDD FLYER'

In the 1950s a fairly frequent passenger service network was operated by auto-train between Pontypridd, the Barry main line, St Fagans, Cardiff, Penarth and Coryton, over railways formerly owned by the Barry, the GW, the Taff Vale, the Rhymney and the Cardiff railway companies. The movement of one such unit over a working day is traced in the following photographs, with the help of the working timetable and a route map.

Alan confesses, 'One of my earliest colour slides was this study of a tree. "JB" happened to be passing northwards on the Barry Railway main line between Creigiau and Efail Isaf stations, with the middle-day return trip to Pontypridd.' April 1959

Alan recalls his astonishment at first seeing an engine pushing carriages at speed along the main line at some forgotten place and date: 'Auto-trains became favourites of mine, particularly one (the "Pontypridd Flyer") that served my locality in west Cardiff. I took a few photographs of it in black-and-white but towards the end of its days in 1960 I captured it on colour film at many locations. It started its weekdays-only journey at Pontypridd and motive power was provided by Abercynon shed. Inherited from pre-grouping times and seemingly exclusive to south Wales, a "target" system was used to identify train workings, this taking the form of a disk fitted to the front of the locomotive bearing letters and numbers or pairs of letters. Abercynon was allocated the letter J and this particular train was sub-lettered B, so it was known to all as "JB". I am indebted to Chris Foren of Bedford for compiling the following extract of "JB"'s movements from the BR Working Timetable showing the quite convoluted pattern of its duties which can be followed on my route sketch. Some station departures were timed to the half-minute.'

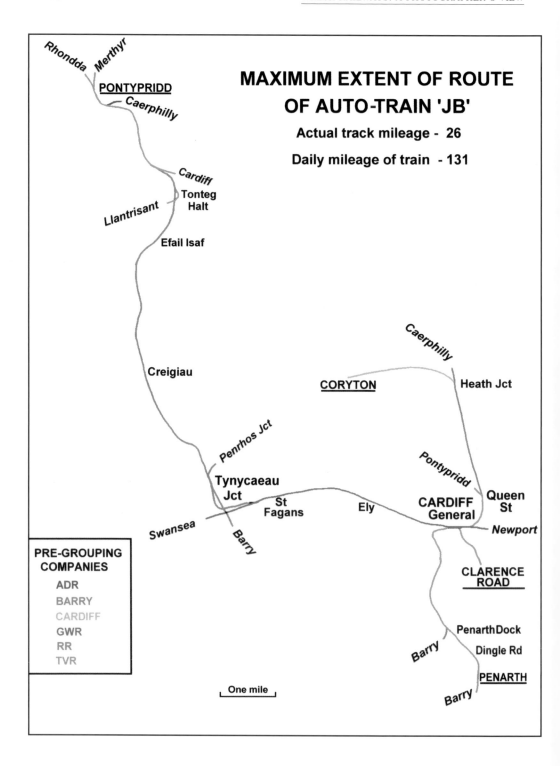

MAXIMUM EXTENT OF ROUTE
OF AUTO-TRAIN 'JB'

Actual track mileage - 26

Daily mileage of train - 131

Rhondda Merthyr

PONTYPRIDD

Caerphilly

Cardiff

Tonteg Halt

Llantrisant

Efail Isaf

Creigiau

Caerphilly

CORYTON   Heath Jct

Penrhos Jct

Pontypridd

Tynycaeau Jct

St Fagans   Ely   **CARDIFF General**   **Queen St**

Swansea   Barry   Newport

CLARENCE ROAD

PenarthDock

Barry   Dingle Rd

PENARTH

Barry

PRE-GROUPING COMPANIES

ADR
BARRY
CARDIFF
GWR
RR
TVR

One mile

THE LIFE AND TIMES OF AUTO-TRAIN JB 21-9-1953 TO 9-9-1960

Light engine depart Abercynon shed 7.16am, arrive Pontypridd 7.23am for duty JB

	am	am	am	am	PM	PM	PM	PM	PM
Pontypridd	7.46	...	...	...	...	1.39	...	...	...
Treforest	7.49	...	...	...	...	1.42	...	...	...
Tonteg	7.54½	...	...	...	...	1.47½	...	...	...
Efail Isaf	7.58	...	...	...	...	1.52	...	...	...
Creigiau	8.04	...	...	...	...	1.57	...	...	...
St Fagans	8.14	...	...	...	...	2.07	...	...	...
Ely Main Line	8.19	...	...	...	...	2.12	...	...	...
Penarth	...	9.13	...	10.40*	12.23	...	2.52	3.52	5.12
Dingle Rd	...	9.15	...	10.42	12.25	...	2.54	3.54	5.14
Penarth Dock	...	...	...	...	12.27	...	...	...	...
Grangetown	...	9.20½	...	10.48	12.31	...	3.00	4.00	5.20
Cardiff General	8.26	9.24½	9.53	10.52	12.35	2.17	3.03½	4.04	5.24
Clarence Road	8.30	9.33	9.56	...	12.39	2E22	3E08	4E09	5E28
Queen Street	...	...	...	10.58	...	...	...	...	...
Coryton	...	...	...	11.14	...	...	...	...	...
Coryton	...	...	...	11.25*	...	...	...	...	...
Queen Street	...	...	...	11.43	...	...	...	...	...
Clarence Road	8.35	9.39	10.03	...	12.45	2E25	3E12	4E34	5E31
Cardiff General	8.41	9.42	10.15	11.48	12.50	2.33	3.20	4.50	5.38
Grangetown	8.45	...	10.19	11.52	...	2.37	3.24	4.54	...
Penarth Dock	...	...	...	...	...	...	...	...	...
Dingle Road	8.55	...	10.25	11.58	...	2.43	3.30	5.00	...
Penarth	8.57	...	10.27	12.00	...	2.45	3.32	5.02	...
Ely Main Line	...	...	...	...	12.55	...	...	...	5.43½
St Fagans	...	...	...	...	1.00	...	...	...	5.48
Creigiau	...	...	...	...	1.09½	...	...	...	6.01½
Efail Isaf	...	...	...	...	1.15	...	...	...	6.07½
Tonteg	...	...	...	...	1.18½	...	...	...	6.12
Treforest	...	...	...	...	1.23½	...	...	...	6.19
Pontypridd	...	...	...	...	1.26½	...	...	...	6.23

Light engine depart Pontypridd 6.35pm, arrive Abercynon 6.42pm for shed

Notes: * Penarth-Coryton-Penarth segment withdrawn with effect from 30 June 1958
    E Saturdays excepted.
    There was no Sunday service.

Weekday service route 7.46am to 6.23pm including Coryton branch, ('Cardiff' indicates General Station):-

Pontypridd, St Fagans, Cardiff, Clarence Rd, Cardiff, Penarth, Cardiff, Clarence Rd, Cardiff, Clarence Rd, Cardiff, Penarth, Cardiff, Queen St, Coryton, Queen Street, Cardiff, Penarth, Cardiff, Clarence Rd, Cardiff, St Fagans, Pontypridd, St Fagans, Cardiff, Clarence Rd, Cardiff, Penarth, Cardiff, Clarence Rd, Cardiff, Penarth, Cardiff, Clarence Rd, Cardiff, Penarth, Cardiff, Clarence Rd, Cardiff, St Fagans, Pontypridd.

Locomotive on last day of service was No. 6438.

Heading northwards on the Barry main line the driver will have noted that the Creigiau distant signal is indicating a clear road ahead beyond the station. September 1960

Viewed from a farm accommodation bridge to the west of St Fagans, 'JB' is on the last run of the day and heading home to Pontypridd. The GWR main line is to the right, with St Fagans station in the distance. September 1960

Propelling its train towards Cardiff, No. 6435 is about to leave St Fagans station in June 1960. The lamp below the chimney is the tail lamp, in the wrong place as such but in the right position to serve as a 'stopping passenger train' head code when running in the other direction. The station building is an original South Wales Railway structure dating from 1872 but the National Museum of Wales, with a presence at nearby St Fagans Castle, seemed uninterested when demolition commenced soon after the station was closed in September 1962.

Leaving St Fagans at 1.00pm 'JB''s fireman leans out to collect from its trackside holder the token authorising the driver to proceed on to the single line section leading up to the Barry main line at Tyn-y-Caeau Junction. August 1959

Entering Ely (Main Line) station, the 1.39pm from Pontypridd is being propelled by No. 6411. 26 September 1953

This photograph was taken from the same position as above, looking in the opposite direction. Business seems brisk as 'JB' pulls up at the platform. 26 September 1953

Viewed from the window of Leckwith Junction signal-box, 'JB' has the Ely distant signal at clear and will make good speed down the main line towards Ely station. The box-to-box bell code for this train on the main line was 5-pause-1. April 1960

Another view from the window of Leckwith Junction signal-box as the train heads towards Ely. The tracks coming in from the left are the connection from the Taff Vale line to Radyr via Waterhall. Normally for freight only, they were used for football trains from the west to Ninian Park Halt. April 1960

The once-daily trip to Coryton ceased on 28 June 1958. Propelled by No. 6435 the 11.25am departure from Coryton is seen joining the Rhymney line from Caerphilly at Heath Junction. 26 August 1953

Clarence Road station, in Cardiff's dock area, was the terminus of the Riverside branch from Cardiff General and was the shortest of 'JB''s four tentacles with eight weekday arrivals and departures. A railwayman boards the train for a ride 'on the cushions' as the fireman mounts the footplate. June 1960

Under the watchful eye of the signalman at Cogan Junction, 'JB' is about to climb Dingle Bank. The signal at the end of the point rodding controlled the line forming the exit from Penarth Docks. August 1960.

Racing through Penarth Dock station to take a run at Dingle Bank (gradient 1 in 49). 'JB' passed through this station 12 times each day but stopped only once, four minutes after its departure from Penarth, on the 12.23pm service to Cardiff. March 1960.

Dingle Bank extended from Cogan Junction (Penarth Dock station) to Penarth Town station, a distance of one mile. Exactly between these points was Dingle Road, one of four 'suburban' stations in Penarth. Steam and diesel propulsion stand side-by-side one day in June 1960. The height of the runner beans confirms the time of year. Alan also made some sound recordings of 'JB' and the standing start from Dingle Road on the bank up to Penarth seemed promising. Alan relates: 'This was before the days of portable cassette recorders and the recording with my 240v mains-operated machine was only made possible with the assistance of the station master at Penarth who kindly promised to have the platform lights at Dingle Road switched on in broad daylight so that I could remove a bulb and plug in my recorder. When I arrived as arranged, one brilliantly sunny day, all the lights were duly lit on both platforms and, after the removal of a very hot bulb, an excellent recording was made. Similar acts of kindness from various signalmen enabled me to make recordings in other locations in and around Cardiff.'

Arrival at Penarth Town. The train will now reverse out under the bridge and return to the platform on the left. Judging from the shadow, the departure will probably be the last of the day, at 5.12pm. September 1960

The crew enjoy a short rest while awaiting departure from Penarth Town. April 1960

Chapter 3

THE VALLEYS

The valleys of Glamorgan and western Monmouthshire are an unusual topographical pattern, running like the ribs of a fan from the high ground southwards towards the Bristol Channel. They are characterised by steep sides and mountain ridges rising to an altitude of 1,000 to 2,000 feet. Iron ore was first discovered in the upper reaches, together with limestone. A plentiful supply of coal for making coke was also found near the surface, high up at the heads of the valleys. Later, steam coal was found in abundance lower down the valleys, often at great depth. It was fortunate that the lie of the land was such that the transportation of iron and coal to the ports was downhill.

Each valley accommodated at least one railway line while some were served by more than one. Two lines, the LMS Merthyr, Tredegar & Abergavenny (MTA) and the GWR Vale of Neath, crossed east to west linking the valleys laterally. There were also locations where transfer was made from one valley to another in order to avoid the dependence of the collieries on access to only one port. This happened at Penrhos between the Taff and the Rhymney and near Machen between the Rhymney and the Ebbw. The Rhondda tunnel, the longest in south Wales at 3,443 yards, linked the Rhondda and Afan valleys. Until the grouping in 1923 the valley railways were mainly owned by Welsh companies, while two were owned by the LMS; the GWR had a group in Monmouthshire and a further cluster around Tondu. Two were owned jointly by the GWR and the Rhymney. After the grouping the GWR predominated.

For the photographer these lines offered smoke, atmosphere, variety and intense activity. They also provided intriguing railway operations with complex track plans and junctions. The mountains, when not shrouded in smokey mist, made an impressive background, yet even within the valleys themselves, there were remarkable contrasts of rural calm and industrial mayhem.

THE TAFF VALE

The Taff Vale was the first railway in Cardiff, opening in 1841 as a standard gauge line from Merthyr. The railway followed the valley of the eponymous river, squeezing its way through the narrow pass at Taff's Well in the company of the river, the Glamorgan canal and later the Cardiff Railway.

North of Pontypridd the valley is first joined by the Cynon and then by the Rhondda. This meant that much of the coal from these prodigious sources, together with the trade of Merthyr and Dowlais, was funnelled through Pontypridd. More than 150 trains a day passed through here in each direction. One third of them were passenger trains and of the rest nearly all were carrying coal. At the peak in 1913, when Cardiff exported some 11 million tons of coal, about 8 million tons of this passed through Pontypridd.

The Taff Vale's first passenger station in Cardiff was close to the important commercial centre near Queen Street; the line was then extended to Bute Road in the docks area. A branch served the Bute West Dock, which had been opened in 1839. Increasing traffic called for the routes to be diversified and the docks extended; accordingly, Bute East Docks was opened in 1858. A new branch to rival docks at Penarth was opened in 1865. This left the main line at Radyr on the northern outskirts of Cardiff where extensive sidings were established for the reception of coal trains and the formation of trains of empties. Later, in 1887, a new line was opened to the Roath Dock on the south-east side of the city. This left the Taff Vale main line south of Radyr at Roath Branch Junction and crossed the eastern suburbs partly on an elevated section.

A sister to the auto-train 'JB', recalled in chapter 2, was 'JF' which ran between Pontypridd and Caerphilly. It is seen here at Pontypridd station in 1955.

The railway spelling of the township of Taff's Well has varied over the years. Taffswell signal-box was situated nearly a mile to the north of Taff's Well station. It was previously named Taffs Well Sidings and before that Taffs Well Junction. What is now Railtrack's Taff's Well station was: from 1840 Taffs Well; from 1863 Walnut Tree Junction; and from 1886 Walnut Tree Bridge. In 1900 it reverted to Taff's Well.
17 May 1964

Two alternative spellings are shown in the window panels and on the seat in this view. The Taff Vale Railway did not normally embellish its stations to this extent. Until its recent lamentable closure the Welsh Industrial and Maritime Museum at Cardiff Pier Head displayed a cast of the decorative panel. The station staff at Taff's Well were able to produce, in 1959, the mandatory (in TVR days) Holy Bible. Its survival was certainly due to the fact that it was kept locked out of sight in the station master's office rather than laid out on the waiting-room table as was the original requirement. Recent investigations have failed to locate any Bibles at former TVR stations. July 1960

At first sight, giving the impression of a super-detailed gauge '00' model layout, this view of the Taff Vale four-track main line was taken from the top of the Walnut Tree viaduct and shows a Class '5600' locomotive, built at a scale of 12 inches to the foot, heading a loaded coal train down the relief line towards Cardiff. At the top right is an arched water main, one of the trunk mains supplying Cardiff from a chain of reservoirs in the Brecon Beacons. This crosses the abandoned Glamorganshire canal at this point. 4 June 1965.

A diesel multiple unit has just passed under the Walnut Tree viaduct on its way to Cardiff. The dense growth beyond the train conceals the route of the former Cardiff Railway. 25 May 1963

Home-going commuters fill the late afternoon train to Treherbert, which is about to pull away from Llandaff station as a Barry-bound diesel multiple unit arrives. No. 5600 was the first of a class of 200 0-6-2T locomotives which handled most of the passenger trains in the valleys. The 0-6-2 wheel arrangement for tank locomotives was particularly well suited to the railway characteristics of south Wales and all the main pre-grouping companies used them. The GWR '5600' Class perpetuated the design. Almost invariably the engines worked chimney-first up the valleys. This was to reduce the risk of the firebox crown in the boiler becoming dry when steaming hard on a rising gradient when running in reverse. 7 June 1962

At Roath Branch Junction, about one mile south of Llandaff station, this view is looking south along the four-track Taff Vale main line towards Cardiff Queen Street station. The Roath branch leads off to the left and on each side of the running lines, for some distance, were extensive storage sidings for coal wagons, both loaded awaiting their turn for off-loading into ships in the docks and empty for return to the collieries. April 1961

Two members of the 0-6-2T '5600' Class stand in the February sunshine outside Radyr shed in 1962. No. 6699, on the left, was the last of the class to be built. Quite a large number of GWR locomotives were built by contractors in the years between the two world wars and Nos. 6650 to 6699 were amongst them. They were constructed by Armstrong Whitworth in 1928. Radyr shed was still standing in 2002.

A distinguished visitor at Radyr shed on 18 March 1964 was ex-LNER 4-6-2 No. 4472 *Flying Scotsman*. It had conveyed its then owner, Alan Pegler, from Doncaster to Cardiff to receive an award for services to tourism in Wales in recognition of his work on the Ffestiniog Railway. During the ceremony No. 4472 was taken to Radyr for servicing and replenishment of coal and water.

There were two Waterhall Junctions and signal-boxes in south Wales. One was on the former Port Talbot Railway in the Pyle area. The TVR signal-box in this photograph is in western Cardiff and it controlled the junction of the Llantrisant No.1 branch with the Taff Vale's Radyr branch, which afforded a direct route from Radyr to the docks at Penarth. Class '5600' No. 6626 has paused outside the box on its way to Radyr. The white board improved the visibility of the signal from approaching trains. June 1960

A '5600' Class 0-6-2T approaches Waterhall Junction from the south on 25 May 1963.

Rosebay willow-herb flourishes on the embankment to the north of Waterhall Junction as an empty wagon train heads for Radyr. The '5600' Class locomotive has lost its smokebox number plate – a sign of the times as the end of the steam era approached. 5 August 1964

An engine and van in the cutting to the south of Waterhall Junction pass the 'down' starting signal which is sited on the right of the track for better observation. 25 May 1963

The cutting to the south of Waterhall Junction 25 years later. Now known as the 'City Line', the former normally freight-only Radyr branch has been furnished with three new stations in the western suburbs of Cardiff. In the absence of sparks from steam locomotives, trees have been allowed to flourish around Fairwater station.

Heading a Leicester to Barry Island day excursion train, an unidentified 'Hall' heads out of Cardiff General past the West signal-box and crosses on to former Taff Vale metals on the final leg of its journey to the seaside. The train will diverge on to Barry Railway metals at Cogan Junction. 30 June 1963

THE RHYMNEY RAILWAY AND THE LAST LINE TO DOWLAIS

The Rhymney Railway set out to convey coal from the Rhymney valley to the docks at Cardiff. However, its coat-of-arms included the arms of the town of Newport, so this must have been intended as an alternative, though it was never reached. Access to Cardiff was initially over the Taff Vale from Walnut Tree Junction, just north of Taff's Well, but congestion and consequent difficulties with the Taff Vale caused the Rhymney to build its Cardiff direct line, completed in 1871. This left the original line at Aber Branch Junction near Caerphilly and then pushed through a tunnel under Caerphilly Mountain and crossed the centre of Cardiff to reach the Bute East Dock. North of Aber, at Hengoed in the Rhymney valley, the Rhymney passed under the Taff Vale Extension of the Newport, Abergavenny & Hereford Railway (later known by the GWR as the Vale of Neath line). Here a physical connection was made at a complicated junction. This enabled LNWR traffic from the Sirhowy valley to be channelled on to the Rhymney for Cardiff. The Rhymney also had a branch leading up the Senghennydd valley from Aber Branch Junction. Later, in an unusual partnership with the GWR, it built branches from Quakers Yard in the Taff valley to Merthyr and from Nelson up the Bargoed Taff valley to Dowlais.

An unusual view of a coal train proceeding up the valley. No. 5683 is on the former Rhymney Railway main line between Ystrad Mynach and Hengoed. The line to the right connected the RR to the Vale of Neath line and was built to enable LNWR trains from the Sirhowy valley to gain access to Cardiff. 30 June 1962.

The 'Rambling 56' rail tour, referred to elsewhere in the following pages, departs southward from Bargoed station. Bargoed colliery and its associated waste tip (then said to be the largest in the country but now completely removed) dominate the background. August 1965.

A '5600' Class is on the crossover on the truncated joint GWR/RR line to Merthyr Tydfil at Quakers Yard High Level. The line was closed above this point in 1951. To the left, the GWR Vale of Neath line becomes single to pass through the nearly half-mile long Cefn Glas tunnel. The red bus is on the old A470 Cardiff – Merthyr – Brecon trunk road. 31 March 1962

No. 9682 enters Caerphilly station from the west. 4 June 1965

No. 343, an ex-TVR Class A 0-6-2T brings the 1.15pm from Coryton on to the Rhymney Railway at Heath Junction. The line in the left foreground would have been part of the line projected, but never built, to a junction with the TVR on the Roath branch. 9 July 1953

64 minutes later the empty Royal Train hauled by 'Castles' Nos. 5006 *Tregenna Castle* and 5080 *Defiant* makes its way up the Rhymney line heading for Ystrad Mynach to pick-up Her Majesty Queen Elizabeth II during her post-accession tour of the UK. 9 July 1953

In the branch platform at Nelson & Llancaiach, No. 5660 awaits its departure over the joint
GW/RR line for Dowlais Cae Harris. September 1963

The landscape from a train near Bedlinog. The line was single by this time. September 1963

In August 1965 the Monmouthshire Railway Society's 'Rambling 56' rail tour train is seen climbing past Bedlinog. The singling of the track had proceeded one stage further.

Approaching Cwmbargoed out on the open moor with a long line of wagons in the distant sidings. September 1963

No. 5672 propels its brake van towards Dowlais Cae Harris to collect its train. 28 April 1962

No. 5635 is midway between Cwmbargoed and Dowlais with a midday passenger train. 28 April 1962

No. 5635 entering Cwm-
bargoed with the return
passenger working to
Nelson. 28 April 1962

A   former   RR   somersault
shunting signal at Cwmbargoed.
28 April 1962

No. 5635 leaving Cwmbargoed for Nelson. 28 April 1962

Arriving at Dowlais Cae Harris. The lines on the left provided access to Dowlais steelworks. September 1963

Cae Harris was one of two terminal stations in the hilltop steel town of Dowlais. September 1963

No. 5660 is about to run around its train in readiness for the return trip to Nelson. September 1963

Barry Railway Infrastructure

The Barry Railway was a late nineteenth-century phenomenon which appeared to break many laws of commerce and economics. It was owned by a company which was primarily a dock owner and which had been founded to provide additional competitive coal exporting facilities. There was therefore an incentive to attract business. In its hunger for coal trade, it built lines like tentacles into the territory of other companies, at great expense and in some cases duplicating existing lines. Nevertheless, in spite of being a latecomer, with its first train arriving as late as 1889, it became extremely profitable and by 1911 enabled the port of Barry to equal Cardiff's coal exports. Against the disadvantage of being a newcomer and having to make heavy investment in infrastructure, the Barry had a modern port, a simple command structure and a favourable location, closer to the main shipping routes than either Cardiff or Newport.

However, when the coal trade started its long decline, the Barry lines were the first to be made redundant. This record is therefore of special value as it focusses on a short-lived phenomenon. The Barry may have arrived late on the scene but it built its plant as though it was to last forever. Its stations were spacious and well equipped. Its signal-boxes were elegant. Its bridges and viaducts were built to high specifications with the best materials. Like the Great Central's London extension, it was a high-quality operation and benefitted from being newly built. Its fate was, however, similar.

Efail Isaf station, in common with other Barry Railway stations, boasted four tracks. This allowed the all-important coal trains to have precedence over passenger trains, which the Barry Company regarded as a secondary source of revenue. In September 1960 the 1.39pm departure from Pontypridd, in the form of auto-train 'JB', pauses here on its journey down to Cardiff.

The attractive but slightly shabby exterior of the station at Creigiau at the time of withdrawal of passenger services. 9 September 1962

An original Barry Railway enamel station name-board.

Regular and occasional summer Sunday excursion trains ran to Barry Island during the 1950s and '60s from places near and far; Leicester being one of the more distant examples. One regular such working was from Nantybwch at the top of the Sirhowy valley in former LNWR territory. This was, more often than not, appropriately hauled by one of the ex-LNWR Class G2 'Super D' 0-8-0 locomotives based at Abergavenny. It is seen here in August 1955 on the evening return journey passing Tyn-y-caeau Junction signal-box and turning on to the Penrhos branch. After crossing Walnut Tree viaduct it will pass through Penrhos Junction and reach Nantybwch by way of Ystrad Mynach, Hengoed and Pontllanfraith. The field at the left of the picture is thought to be the site of the Battle of St Fagans in 1648 in which the local Parliamentarian army soundly routed the forces of King Charles I.

Alan remembers: 'I had spent an hour one August evening in 1962 photographing the procession of return Barry Island excursions at this location (now buried under the Cardiff Bay – M4 link road) and was making good progress along the sleepers to reach my parked motor cycle when I heard an eager panting and was confronted by an enthusiastic Alsatian dog. "Keep quite still", came a voice from the bushes, which was superfluous as I had already frozen. Then appeared a very pleasant young member of the Glamorgan Police. Tethering his pet, he eyed my camera and, making no reference to my forty shillings' worth of trespass, invited me back to his cottage in St Fagans where his benevolent mother provided tea and cake as he showed me his album of railway photographs, many taken from precisely the same spot that I had been using.

'During one of my earlier evening visits I had noticed that several of the trains had crawled past the signal-box having been slowed by the signalman leaving his signals at "danger" for no apparent reason. I later discovered that when a signalman down the line espied a courting couple in an otherwise empty non-corridor compartment, it was his practice to telephone his colleague ahead who would then slow the train until it was close by, the better to observe what was going on in the compartment, its position in the train having been advised.'

An April 1962 study of Drope Junction signal-box on the Barry main line. The lines to the left make a connection with the GWR main line at Peterston. This connection was closed one month before the Barry main line which itself was completely closed on 31 March 1963, passenger services having been withdrawn in September 1962.

On the Barry main line at Drope Junction 0-6-2T No. 5691 heads towards Barry with a coal train, probably for Aberthaw power station, a few days before closure of the line. The train has crossed two viaducts, one over the GWR main line and the connecting chord line to the Barry at Tyn-y-Caeau Junction and the other over the river Ely. The chimney-stack beyond the signal-box is all that remains of the Barry Railway pumping station which lifted water from the river and supplied the large header tank and water columns nearby, as illustrated in the next picture. A dual carriageway now occupies the trackbed. 12 April 1963.

The train will soon enter the 1,867-yard Wenvoe tunnel. After closure the tunnel was used for water-supply purposes, the local water undertaking having laid a large diameter water main through it to augment supplies to the Barry area. 12 April 1963

Still *in situ* a year after traffic ceased was this rotating ground signal at Wenvoe. The aspect of this piece of original equipment was changed by rotating the red/green box containing lenses and an oil lamp about its vertical axis. Later practice was to use a disc as a miniature semaphore signal. 27 March 1964

The principal engineering work on the Vale of Glamorgan section of the Barry Railway was the viaduct at Porthkerry with a length of 374 yards. Two '5600' Class 0-6-2Ts head a coal train for Aberthaw power station on 30 August 1962. Unlike most of the infrastructure of the Barry Railway, this viaduct was poorly constructed and partially collapsed twice in 1896 while under construction and again in 1898 six weeks after the line was opened. A 2½ mile temporary diversion had to be built, following a tortuous route to keep to the contour of the land. Full traffic over the viaduct recommenced in April 1900 and has continued ever since.

A view looking down on to the viaduct was available from the churchyard at Porthkerry. Another coal train is heading for Aberthaw on 19 May 1964. It is hauled by an 0-6-2T, this time assisted in the rear by another member of the class.

Approaching Aberthaw, the Vale of Glamorgan line ran along the top of the cliffs. At the foot of the cliffs was the site of the former terminus of the Taff Vale Railway branch from Llantrisant via Cowbridge. Yet another train for the power station approaches on 26 March 1964. A cow appears to be dicing with death at the edge of the cliff.

Llandow signal-box was sited on the top of the cutting for better observation of traffic. This required all the signal wires to pass around two sets of pulley wheels and the point rodding to change direction twice. A similar state of affairs existed at nearby Gileston. March 1961

A typical Barry Railway somersault signal is sited at the top of the embankment at Llandow to lengthen its sighting by an approaching train. March 1961

A little before sunset on a bright day in March 1961, a homeward-bound ballast train saunters through Llandow on the Vale of Glamorgan line.

In August 1965 the Monmouthshire Railway Society ran a rail tour, 'The Rambling 56', hauled by '5600' Class No. 6643. It was centred mainly on lines of the Rhymney Railway but is seen here on ex-Barry metals as it returns from Walnut Tree viaduct to Penrhos Junction. Nantgarw colliery is in the background and the tracks serving it are on the original trackbed of the Cardiff Railway, a connection to the Taff Vale at Taff's Well being made in June 1952. The appearance of a coach in Southern Region green begs the question whether any other such coach ever passed over Walnut Tree viaduct.

LINES TO PENRHOS JUNCTION

Penrhos Junction lay at a crossing point between the Taff and Rhymney valleys. At this point the mountain ridge between the two valleys is lower and it was possible to make a rail link without having to build a tunnel. Nevertheless, a deep cutting was required and the photographer had the benefit of a road bridge conveniently built across the middle of it. Through this cutting the Rhymney Railway built its original main line in 1858, descending from the north-east down the Rhymney valley and making contact with the Taff Vale Railway at Taff's Well. This necessitated a descent down a 1:47 gradient towards the south-west, known locally as the 'Big Hill'. Until 1871 this was its only access to Cardiff.

The next occupant of the saddle between the two valleys was the Pontypridd, Caerphilly & Newport Railway (PC & N). This was a line built to create a new link between the Glamorganshire coalfield and the port of Newport. It was promoted by the Alexandra Docks & Railway Company (ADR). This approached Penrhos from Pontypridd to the north-west and proceeded in an easterly direction to Caerphilly over the Rhymney, and then over the Brecon & Merthyr to Newport.

The third and final occupant was the Barry Railway which, in 1901, established a link with the Rhymney in the Penrhos cutting with a line which had crossed the Taff on a major viaduct known as the Walnut Tree viaduct. This enabled coal from the Rhymney valley to be diverted to the new port of Barry.

In 1905 the Barry Railway built an expensive connection to the Brecon & Merthyr Railway by building a viaduct across the cutting at Penrhos from its existing line and heading north-east across two more viaducts, Penyrheol and Llanbradach, and thus across the Rhymney river to the Brecon & Merthyr on the far side of the valley.

'6400' Class pannier tank No. 6435 is in 'pull' mode as it pauses with its auto-train at Dynea Halt on the Alexandra Docks & Railway Company line from Pontypridd to Caerphilly. Penrhos Junction lies four miles ahead. 1955

Penrhos Junction was in fact a collective name for four junctions. From the south, Penrhos Lower was the junction of the two Barry lines where the 1905 extension to the B & M left the original line built to join the Rhymney in 1901. The link between the Barry 1901 line and the Rhymney was effected at Penrhos South. Immediately east, the PC & N line from Pontypridd joined the Rhymney at Walnut Tree Branch Junction. Just beyond that, the Rhymney lines split at Beddau Branch Junction, left and north for Rhymney, straight-on for Caerphilly. The part of the cutting west of the road bridge survives but is largely overgrown, with a profusion of silver birch trees. The eastern half is filled-in and covered by a housing estate.

There were three more halts on this line before Caerphilly was reached, these being Upper Boat, Groeswen and Nantgarw. Groeswen halt was typical and shows the quite primitive facilities. Another auto-train pulls away towards Penrhos Junction. 1955

On the original Rhymney Railway line 0-6-2T No. 5621 tackles the 'Big Hill' from the junction with the Taff Vale at Walnut Tree (Taff's Well) to Penrhos Junction. The Barry Railway Walnut Tree viaduct can be seen in the background. 22 April 1963

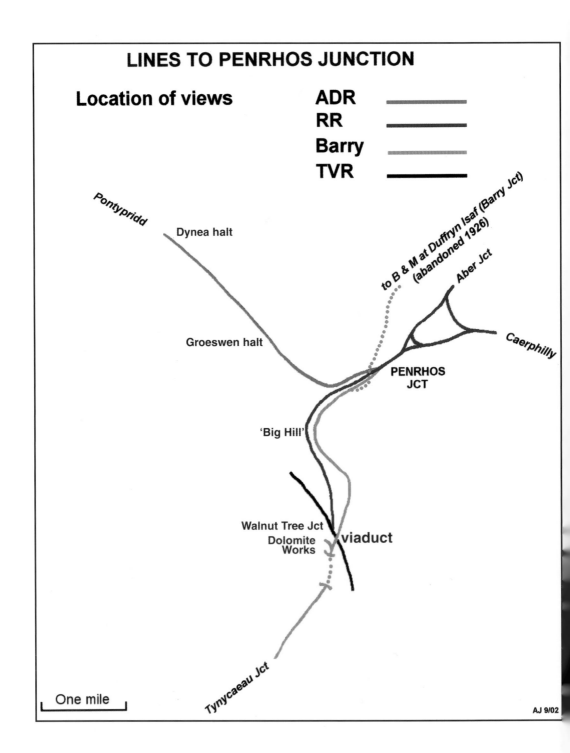

LINES TO PENRHOS JUNCTION

Location of views

ADR
RR
Barry
TVR

Pontypridd

Dynea halt

to B & M at Duffryn Isaf (Barry Jct)
(abandoned 1926)

Aber Jct

Groeswen halt

Caerphilly

PENRHOS
JCT

'Big Hill'

Walnut Tree Jct
Dolomite
Works

viaduct

Tynycaeau Jct

One mile

AJ 9/02

A brilliantly sunny evening in July 1964 sees another 0-6-2T No. 5670 trundling its brake van northwards past Rockwood signal-box and heading towards Penrhos Junction.

The Barry Railway main line and the branch to Penrhos Junction were closed as from 1 April 1963, but the dolomite quarry on the hillside above Taff's Well continued to be served by rail from Penrhos Junction until December 1967. Viewed from the guard's van the train rounds the hillside above Nantgarw on its way to the quarry. This and the next view were obtained by Alan thumbing a lift from the guard as the train trundled past Penrhos Junction signal-box. 4 June 1965

At the quarry '5600' Class No. 6672 prepares to haul wagons out of the loading area. 4 June 1965

Still on ex-Rhymney Railway metals a '5600' Class 0-6-2T reaches the top of the bank and heads north-eastwards past Penrhos Junction signal-box with a short train of empty coal wagons. This was a rare example of a signal-box having block bell communication with five other signal-boxes. There were some instances of this in large city junctions but it was uncommon in the countryside. Alan fondly remembers a large patch of wild strawberries on the nearby embankment. September 1963

In the charge of 0-6-2T No. 5698, a loaded coal train prepares for the cautious descent of the bank down to the TVR main line. In the middle distance can be seen the supports of the Barry Railway viaduct which carried that company's traffic-raiding branch to a junction with the Brecon and Merthyr Railway across the Rhymney valley, opposite Llanbradach. The lines to the left were also Barry Railway and the associated yard, out of sight in the distance, had its moment of glory in 1943. It was used to store some 150 US Army Transportation Corps Class 'S160' 2-8-0 locomotives in readiness for use in Europe, following the Allied invasion in 1944. 27 August 1964

No. 5698 drifts away down the bank, as another locomotive of the same class, assisted in the rear by a banking engine, reaches the top of the climb from Walnut Tree Junction.

As it drops away from the train the banking engine reveals itself. The 0-6-0 pannier tank will now return to Walnut Tree Junction to await its next call for assistance.

A loaded coal train from Pontypridd passes under the road bridge at Penrhos Junction on the metals of the former Pontypridd, Caerphilly and Newport Railway. 31 July 1963

A view to the north-east from the road bridge in September 1963. Coming in from the left is the Pontypridd, Caerphilly and Newport Railway which had been singled by this date. Ahead, the lines to the left lead to Aber Junction and those to the right to Caerphilly station.

Books devoted to 'Then and Now' railway scenes have become popular in recent years. Penrhos Junction has been selected for such treatment in this book. Comparison of these views taken in 1997 with similar views above shows vividly how the landscape can be changed by a new use. To the west of the road bridge nature has so far been allowed to take its course. Things are different on the eastern side however. The cutting and road bridge have been filled in, new houses loom in the camera viewfinder and the only identifying feature is the outline of Mynydd Machen in the distance. August 1997

THE BRECON AND MERTHYR RAILWAY IN MONMOUTHSHIRE

Monmouthshire's character differed markedly either side of the river Usk. West of the river was one of the most heavily industrialised areas in Britain; east and north it was agricultural. Newport, the largest town, had been a walled town with a castle from about 1100. It is situated near the mouth of the Usk which is a non-navigable river. Unlike the valleys of the Tawe and the Taff, the Usk valley did not develop as a channel for industrial products and the river is best known for its fishing. It was the tributaries of the Usk – the Sirhowy, the Ebbw Fawr and Ebbw Fach, the Tyleri and the Llwyd flowing down the western and eastern valleys of Monmouthshire – which played host to both the iron and coal industries. The railways running down these valleys were built on the routes of tramroads, originally laid to carry iron products from the ironworks at the heads of the valleys, at Blaenavon, Sirhowy, Beaufort, Tredegar and Nantyglo, either to canal heads or all the way to Newport. The longest of these tramroads was the Rumney which became part of the Brecon & Merthyr Railway in 1864. It descended the east bank of the Rhymney river while the Rhymney Railway occupied the west bank. Near Machen the escarpment between the Rhymney and Ebbw valleys was low enough to permit the tramroad to cross from one valley to the other, and thus make its way to Newport.

Alan interjects: 'I must thank fellow enthusiast Derek Chaplin for drawing my attention in June 1962 to the photographic possibilities offered by the 7.07pm train from Newport to Brecon. Due to the hilly terrain, photography was only possible for a few weeks either side of midsummer day but the sun co-operated brilliantly on most evenings and from just the right angle. Collett 0-6-0 tender engines Nos. 2218 and 2247 were the usual train engines with pannier tanks providing occasional variety. The views are presented in order travelling north, with a few additional scenes inserted here and there.'

Leaving Newport High Street station on 21 July 1962

The Newport transporter bridge is visible in this view of No. 2247 approaching Park Junction, having left the GWR main line at Gaer Junction and passed through the 403-yard Gaer tunnel. 14 July 1962

Entering Bassaleg station. The train has branched to the left off the GWR at Bassaleg Junction, a quarter of a mile to the rear and is now on B & M metals. 14 June 1962

Pannier tank No. 3766 was in charge on 12 July 1962 and is seen passing the siding at Machen quarry. As at October 2002 the line was still in being from Bassaleg Junction to this point to serve the quarry.

Running into Machen station, junction for the B & M branch towards Caerphilly. The lack of sun here was probably an advantage, preventing the buildings from being thrown into deep shadow. 25 June 1962

A view westward from the junction at Machen. On the right is the main line to Brecon. It is heading west at this point but after Bedwas it will turn northwards along the eastern side of the Rhymney valley, with the Rhymney railway on the western side and both continuing in this way to Bargoed. The lines to the left are the 'up' and 'down' lines of the branch to Caerphilly. For about two miles beyond the junction these lines parted company and were about half-a-mile apart. Thus local passengers for Caerphilly would board the train at Waterloo halt but on their return they would alight at Fountain Bridge halt. 1954

With his hand on the vacuum brake lever in front of him, the driver brings his auto-train from Machen to Caerphilly and Pontypridd to a gentle stand at minimally furnished Waterloo halt. Although some of the fencing appears to have been painted recently, the white poster next to the lamp announces the withdrawal of the service as from 17 September 1956. The photograph was taken a few days earlier.

No. 2218 has passed the junction at Machen, a few chains west of the station. The signal alongside the white house controls traffic from the Caerphilly branch. 9 July 1962

Returning from Brecon on an afternoon train on Christmas Eve 1962 is 0-6-0 pannier tank No. 4611 approaching Machen.

At Bedwas station a somersault signal gives an unequivocal indication. The splendid tapered 'pigeon puzzler' finials topping the signal-posts were quite rare by this time, being made of sheet zinc which had become frangible with age. Sharing the picture is a standard GWR corrugated iron 'pagoda' shelter. October 1962

Shadowed on the retaining wall, pannier tank No. 3647 approaches Trethomas station with a mid-morning New Tredegar train. 22 December 1962

A pannier tank leaves Trethomas with a pick-up freight for Newport. 22 December 1962

No. 2247 passes through the middle of Bedwas colliery while the resident Andrew Barclay NCB locomotive shunts alongside. 19 July 1962

No. 2218 has turned northwards and is running along the east side of the Rhymney valley towards Maesycymmer. It is approaching Duffryn Isaf signal-box. The tracks just visible in the grass on the right are all that remain of the exchange sidings with the Barry Railway, whose branch from the main line at Tyn-y-Caeau Junction terminated here after crossing Llanbradach viaduct. 14 June 1962

Although only a week after the longest day, the light is failing on a dull evening as a northbound train pulls out of Fleur-de-Lis platform at 7.48pm. 30 June 1962

Chapter 4

RURAL WALES

The mood has changed, the pace has slowed down. The massive movement of coal in the dense and complex network of the valleys gives way to the infrequent and relaxed operations of the single track lines of most of the rest of Wales. Here milk churns replace mines, and cattle take over from coal, but the mountains and valleys remain and continue to challenge the railway. The distances are now much greater and are made to seem even longer by the slow speed of progress over winding track with many gradients and frequent stopping places. Most of what is recorded here has gone, even where, as in the case of the old Cambrian main line, passenger services still operate. The leisurely pottering about with small parcels of freight in the hands of more railway workers than passengers has given way to a much more efficient operation with hardly a railwayman in sight, but the charm has largely disappeared.

BALA TO BLAENAU FFESTINIOG

Of the three lines which at one time served Blaenau Ffestiniog, the line from Bala is the only one which has been closed. This is a great pity as it was spectacularly beautiful on a clear day. Over its 25 mile route, mainly across open mountainside, it climbed to a height of 1,278 feet with rarely a human dwelling in sight. A peculiarity of the line was that the last three miles from Ffestiniog to Blaenau Ffestiniog were originally laid to the narrow gauge of the Ffestiniog Railway. When the GWR promoted the line from Bala Junction to Ffestiniog, the older line was bought and converted. The complete line was opened in 1883. In Blaenau Ffestiniog no interchange was made with the former LNWR branch down to Llandudno Junction, though the narrow gauge Ffestiniog Railway did link the two stations. Train services ceased in 1961 but the seven mile section from Blaenau to a now closed nuclear power station at Trawsfynydd has survived, together with the standard gauge later line laid over the narrow gauge connection between the former GWR and LMS stations. Sadly, its future is uncertain.

Alan takes up the narrative: 'The trip to Blaenau Ffestiniog on 18 August 1959 was indeed spectacular as I hope the pictures will show. This was my first experience of the line and my first railway holiday using colour film. I had set out from Cardiff the day before, travelling up the Rhymney Railway to Bargoed, then the Brecon & Merthyr to Talyllyn Junction, the Cambrian to Moat Lane and on to Barmouth, enjoying the stretch poised on the cliff face past Friog. I then turned inland on to the GWR to Bala where I spent the night.

'I had previously visited Blaenau and the Penrhyn and Dinorwig slate quarries in

1953, when steam locomotives occupied every shelf of the workings, so I returned to Bala on the next train, having been promised a footplate ride. I was duly invited on to the footplate at Llan Ffestiniog and asked to return to my coach at Frongoch, the last station before Bala. I was using a Western Region Rail Rover ticket and suddenly decided to head south. The booking-clerk at Bala did not turn a hair when I asked him (at about 4.00pm) to reserve me a berth on that night's sleeping train from Paddington to Penzance, simply picking up his hand-wound telephone and asking Shrewsbury to put him through to Paddington. A berth was available. I paid for it and was issued with a handwritten ticket and then travelled to Birmingham via Shrewsbury, Bridgnorth and Kidderminster, and then on to Paddington where I boarded the sleeper and dawn found me travelling alongside the Exe estuary at Starcross. I then travelled on most of the branch lines in Cornwall and Devon for the rest of the week. I seem to remember that the Rail Rover ticket cost me £15 for a week's travel from Cardiff to Cardiff via Blaenau Ffestiniog, London and Penzance.'

A passenger's view of the train near Frongoch, the first station out from Bala. The train is hauled by 0-6-0PT No. 7403.

The line has now gained considerable height and runs along a ledge cut into the mountainside. The train is nearing Capel Celyn halt at a height of about 1,200 feet above sea level, having climbed some 700 feet in the six-mile journey from Bala at an average gradient of 1 in 45.

About to cross the 159 yard long Blaen-y-cwm viaduct, Cwm Prysor.

Exchanging staff and token at Trawsfynydd, the principal intermediate station and passing loop.

Refreshments at Trawsfynydd.

Approaching Teigl Halt with its 'pagoda' waiting shelter, a design unique to the GWR and used widely.

Near journey's end, approaching the terminus at Blaenau Ffestiniog.

Pannier tank No. 8791 of the '5700' Class is ready to depart on the journey back to Bala.

Another view of Teigl Halt.

The shelf cut into the side of Craig Aderyn seen from the footplate of No. 8791. The line can be followed along the slope of the hills in the distance.

THE CAMBRIAN RAILWAYS

The construction of what became the Cambrian Railways was almost as remarkable as their substantial survival in 2002. Completion of a railway from Shropshire across mid-Wales to the coast of Cardigan Bay was achieved by the spirit and determination of visionary Welsh entrepreneurs. The main line from Whitchurch, a small town on the line from Crewe to Shrewsbury, was completed as far as Machynlleth by four small companies which merged as the Cambrian Railways in 1864. The promoters of a fifth, the Aberystwyth and Welsh Coast, had originally intended to build a line from Aberystwyth up the coast, crossing the river Dyfi on a long viaduct. In 1865 this company merged with the Cambrian, having decided to link Aberystwyth and Machynlleth before building the line northward. This was now pushed along the coast from near Machynlleth and reached Pwllheli in 1867. A branch to Dolgellau met the GWR line from Ruabon with an end-on junction. The final piece in the jig-saw was the Mid-Wales line from Moat Lane Junction to near Brecon which became part of the Cambrian in 1904. This line, following a picturesque route down the upper Wye valley, had been built as part of a tenuous link between the north of England and south Wales. The result of this activity was a mixture of main lines and local services. The distance from Pwllheli to Whitchurch was 125 miles, yet at the same time it was a local line serving schoolchildren and shoppers. In some ways it resembled the lines of the old Highland Railway in Scotland. Like the Highland it provided through carriages and connections for tourists from England and today is similarly dependent on political support.

Barmouth station, looking south. The Cadair Idris range is clearly visible on the skyline. Locomotive No. 6340 heads a northbound train. The large goods shed was built by the GW after the grouping, as the original had to be removed to allow extension of the platforms. 17 August 1959

The Mawddach estuary and the line to Dolgellau. The train from Barmouth Junction is headed by a 2-6-0 locomotive. 17 August 1959

Viewed looking towards Barmouth, Morfa Mawddach signal-box was formerly named Barmouth Junction and controlled the junction with the line from Ruabon and Dolgellau. Passenger services ceased on that line in January 1965 and the rusty rails can be seen entering on the right. September 1966

A southbound goods train, including four gunpowder wagons and hauled by a BR Class 4 4-6-0, has just passed safely through Tywyn station. The sidings at the Wharf station of the Talyllyn Railway can be seen behind the train. September 1966

Dovey Junction and station looking towards Machynlleth. Collett 0-6-0 No. 3208 is proceeding light engine on the loop line towards Aberystwyth, having exchanged tokens at the box. The darker surface at the far end of the platform indicates an extension constructed of wood. 25 July 1959

No. 2281 heads a train for Dovey Junction at Machynlleth. 25 July 1959

The 'down' Cambrian Coast Express at Machynlleth headed by No. 7819 *Hinton Manor*. At this station the train was split, the Aberystwyth portion departing first. The signal-box shown in the previous photograph was removed in 1960 and replaced by a central box. 25 April 1963

Machynlleth top yard with 4-4-0 'Dukedog' No. 9018. 25 July 1959

Cemmes Road station looking east towards Talerddig. The wagons seen through the trees
mark the location of the 6¾-mile long Mawddwy Railway which finally closed on 1 July
1951. 'Mogul' No. 6342 heads a westbound train on 25 July 1959.

Talerddig station with No. 75020, a Standard Class 4, piloting an unidentified 'Manor'. They are heading up the climb towards Welshpool. 25 July 1959

Erwood station looking north. The signalman seems to be holding the token for collection in a most unconventional stance. The locomotive is a 2-6-0 Ivatt Class 2. 17 August 1959

A scene on the Mid-Wales line north of Erwood. 17 August 1959

Three Cocks Junction station with a goods train from the Mid-Wales line being shunted by its locomotive, No. 45622, an Ivatt 2-6-0. These LMS designed locomotives were introduced on the former Cambrian lines to replace ageing GWR 0-6-0s. No. 45622 was one of a batch of 25 such locomotives built by the Western Region at Swindon in 1952 and 1953. 8 June 1962

Three Cocks Junction station with a Moat Lane to Brecon train. The Midland Railway's line from Hereford is on the right. 7 July 1962

South-west of Three Cocks and between Talgarth and Talyllyn Junction was Trefeinon station with a fine display of flowers. The train is heading in the Brecon direction. August 1960

At Talyllyn Junction the Mid-Wales Railway had a station on the Talyllyn loop, the eastern side of the triangle. At this time it was still in use as a dwelling. The train, from Three Cocks Junction, is heading towards the station which replaced it. On departure for Brecon it will enter the Talyllyn tunnel, originally bored by the Hay Railway and opened in 1816. In the background is the north-west escarpment of the Black Mountains. 8 June 1962

Aberystwyth station and the main arrival platform for trains from the Welshpool direction, with standard 2-6-4T No. 80098. To the right can be seen the Carmarthen line platforms. 26 April 1963

Headed by BR Standard 2-6-4T No. 80098, the 10.30am train from Aberystwyth to Whitchurch awaits its departure time. 26 April 1963

This picture calls for some explanation from the photographer: 'I thought that the previous shot was a bit lifeless and decided to wait for the actual departure and a bit of steam, which turned out to be rather more than I had bargained for and not from where I had expected. This was not an act of spite on the part of the driver; he had opened the cylinder drain cocks to eject water which would have collected from condensed steam during the wait. To have moved off without doing this might have resulted in a fractured cylinder-end cover or a bent piston rod, water being incompressible.' 26 April 1963

The 12.30pm departure for Whitchurch behind 'Manor' Class No. 7827 viewed from the Carmarthen line arrival platform. 26 April 1963

ABERYSTWYTH TO CARMARTHEN

Geography created a problem for the promoters of railways at Carmarthen. As was the case at Swansea, the South Wales Railway by-passed the town in its dash for Fishguard, creating in 1852 a station some way to the south, later called Carmarthen Junction. The task of linking this to the town fell to the Carmarthen & Cardigan Railway which was promoted in 1854 to build a line to Cardigan by way of the Gwili valley, Pencader, Llandysul in the Teifi valley, and Newcastle Emlyn. Newcastle Emlyn eventually became the terminus of the line in 1895, by which time the railway had become part of the GWR (in 1881). Carmarthen station was built by the Carmarthen & Cardigan on a site just north of the present station, which replaced the old one in 1902. This created the same difficulty as at Swansea, as trains calling at Carmarthen on their way to and from points west have to reverse. Carmarthen Junction station was closed in 1926.

The section from Pencader through Lampeter and Strata Florida to Aberystwyth was opened progressively by the notoriously ill-named Manchester & Milford Railway in 1866 and 1867. This company was absorbed by the GWR in 1911. The resulting through GWR line from Carmarthen to Aberystwyth survived until 1964. The line was never busy, though the five passenger trains a day had to be reduced to three during the Second World War to accommodate munitions trains in connection with the RN armaments store at Trecŵn near Fishguard.

Aberystwyth was the terminus of three separate railways. The first, which became part of the Cambrian, arrived from the north in 1864. The second, the Manchester & Milford, arrived in 1867 from the south. The third, the narrow gauge Vale of Rheidol, arrived from the east in 1897. A spacious station was developed over the years with the GWR constructing a handsome new building in 1930, but sadly the impressive structure has become seriously surplus to requirements and the remaining platform with its fine canopies now seems somewhat desolate.

Alan recalls: 'Even before publication of the Beeching Report in March 1963 there was a general feeling that many little-used branch lines and duplicated main lines could not survive the advance of the private car and road freight transport, and the need to record these routes on film became increasingly urgent. On the following pages are several sets of photographs taken on one or more outings to particular lines. Coupled with the need to photograph as many lineside locations as possible was a natural desire to travel on the line and these two aims could not be achieved simultaneously. Travelling on the line meant a quick dash along the platform at each stop (made easier if a trip on the footplate had been granted by a kind driver) but the end result was a camera full of head-on views of the locomotive with bits of some of the stations also included in the scene. Further visits to the line by motor cycle were necessary to hunt out scenic or typical locations. Such views are also included.'

Scenes from a journey on 26 April 1963: Alan was invited on to the locomotive footplate at the first station stop after Aberystwyth and remained there until the last stop before Carmarthen.

Aberystwyth station. 'The 11.55am train to Carmarthen will depart from platform 1.' It will be hauled by Collett 0-6-0 No. 2224.

Caradog Falls halt looking north along one of the few stretches of straight line.

Caradog Falls halt looking south with a train for Aberystwyth which has just emerged from the 86 yard long Tynygraig tunnel.

Strata Florida was so-called by an English management mishearing the Welsh name Ystrad Fflur. In this view of the station, looking north, the line to Aberystwyth curves away to the west just where it was the original intention of the Manchester & Milford to head straight on behind the station to Llanidloes, beyond the distant mountains. Originally intended to be on a branch off the 'main line', Aberystwyth became the northern terminus in August 1867.

The station at Tregaron. This section of the line crossed an immense bog, Cors Caron, which presented stability problems during and after construction.

The approach to Pontllanio station seen from the footplate. The clutter on the platform, typical of a rural station, gives a spurious impression of activity.

A busy afternoon at Lampeter.

The box at Llanybyther, a place famous for its horse sales. In the siding is a train of 'Presflo' concrete wagons.

Llanpumpsaint station signal-box.

Homeward-bound permanent way man at Conwil.

'Manor' Class No. 7811 *Dunley Manor* heads a Fishguard-bound train at Carmarthen. On the middle road are two travelling Post Office carriages with off-centre corridor connections.

THE CARDIGAN BRANCH

Authorised in 1869 to link slate quarries at Glog with the south Wales main line at Whitland, this little branch was opened progressively, eventually reaching Cardigan in 1886. Because it crossed the eastern end of the Presely Hills the railway was severely graded with a climb northward to the summit at Crymmych Arms, at the head of the Taf valley, at gradients ranging from 1 in 35 to 1 in 50. It then descended at 1 in 40. Cardigan was the classic branch line terminus. It closed in 1963.

The following photographs were taken on 16 June 1962 during a journey along the branch with a group of friends. The single coach train was the 11.35am from Whitland, hauled by 0-6-0 PT No. 1666.

Llanglydwen station, the first of three passing loops on the single line branch.

A study of the end of a Hawksworth brake third coach at Rhydowen.

Boncath, the busiest station on the line, boasted a quite extensive goods yard as well as the second passing loop.

Kilgerran. The line has now dropped down into the Teifi valley. Three miles to go to reach Cardigan.

Cardigan town was on the opposite bank of the river from the station. The line here runs alongside the river.

Although only one year away from closure, Cardigan station appears to be quite busy. A GWR Class '4500' 2-6-2T simmers outside the sub-shed and a variety of freight awaits loading or collection.

Running alongside the Teifi estuary No. 4557 passes the starting signal as it approaches the station.

Chapter 5

INDUSTRIAL RAILWAYS

Handmaidens to the main railways were the miles of low-grade track operating in the collieries and works. South Wales experienced a massive concentration of heaving industrial activity, nearly all crammed into the narrow valleys. Now that it has almost completely disappeared, the once too familiar images of smoke, black dust, grime and ironwork have become only a memory, almost unimaginable. The pithead gear, engine houses, blast-furnaces, chimneys and enormous slag heaps have been bulldozed away. The mineral lines which wound their way into these complexes to feed them raw materials and drag away their products have also gone.

Not immediately captivating and far from glamorous, the industrial lines nevertheless had an appeal. They could not compete with the excitement and speed associated with express passenger trains, with the glamour and size of a main line locomotive, even with the labouring, ponderous progress of a long-distance freight train. But they had character. This stemmed partly from their locomotives which were varied and often quaint, partly from the men who knew them so well, and partly from the violence and intensity of the activities inside the immense factory complexes. There was poetry in the contrasts between industry and the mountain landscape.

Alan takes up the narrative: 'Unsurprisingly, the bulk of my collection of Welsh industrial railway scenes is from south Wales, mainly the collieries and steelworks. In the early 1950s John Wiltshire, another Cardiff railway enthusiast, introduced me to the world of industrial railways and provided details of the many locations where industrial locomotives were to be found and accompanied me on many subsequent photographic trips. In those days there was scant regard for "Health and Safety" (the expression hadn't come into official use) and, except at a few places, one could wander, unchallenged, into colliery yards and steelworks sidings and even into the actual operational areas. High-visibility orange vests and hard hats were almost unknown although locomotives were starting to be disfigured with "wasp stripes". Two extreme examples of my foolhardiness or intrepidity, whichever they may be considered to be, are included in this collection. In one location I was alone, in the other with an informal party, but in neither was there any challenge from workers or officials.

'I arrived at one rural location to find the locomotive parked between two small sheds. The driver and shunter were both sitting on the grass in the sun, partaking of their grub, so I decided to wait until operations resumed, realising that this might not be too immediate. But then I was invited to move the locomotive myself to a position more suitable for photography "and please bring it back when you've finished".'

(Opposite, bottom)   Amid the mountains and slate waste heaps of Blaenau Ffestiniog lived this curious 2 ft gauge machine at J.W. Greaves & Sons' slate quarry. *The Eclipse* was a conversion to 220v dc overhead electric operation of a Bagnall 0-4-0 saddle tank

Emerald Isle, a Bristol-built Peckett 0-6-0 saddle tank of 1916, approaches the entrance to the Melingriffith Tin-plate Works of the Steel Company of Wales at Whitchurch, Cardiff on the private railway converted from a narrow gauge tramway in 1877. The line skirted the river Taff, crossing the TVR main line on the level at Pentyrch Crossing, and led to the Pentyrch ironworks and lime kilns at the foot of the Little Garth Hill. It once ran on to connect with the TVR at Taffswell Sidings signal-box featured in chapter 3. 16 April 1953

locomotive of 1899. The date of the on-site conversion is thought to be around 1927, which accords with the facts that there was an eclipse of the sun shortly after sunrise on 27 June 1927 and Blaenau Ffestiniog was close to the path of totality. Another locomotive, similarly converted in 1930, was named *The Coalition* to reflect the composition of the Ramsey MacDonald government at the time. 18 August 1952

Bristol-built in 1906 by the Avonside Engine Co. 0-6-0 saddle tank No. 1512 hauls wagons from the steelworks at Pontymister past 'The Rolling Mill' public house on its way to the main line near Risca station. 5 April 1954.

Adams' Yard in Newport was something of a mecca for industrial locomotive enthusiasts. A.R. Adams and Son were in the business of buying, selling, repairing and breaking-up such locomotives and kept a small working stock for hire to firms whose own were in for repair. There was usually something fresh to be seen on every visit. *Trevor* was a 2' 6" gauge 0-4-0 saddle-tank-plus-tender locomotive built by Bagnall in 1899. It spent much of its working life with the Manchester Corporation Cleansing Department at Irlam, Lancs., eventually arriving at Adams' Yard in 1944. Dismantling started in 1949 but it was a lingering death. It was photographed in 1954 and was finally put down in the following year.

0-4-0 saddle tank *Mary* is seen shunting at the premises of Coast Lines Ltd at Moderator Wharf on the west bank of the river Usk at Newport, close to the transporter bridge. Built in 1888 by Hudswell Clark of Leeds, *Mary* was previously employed at Bedford Gasworks and reached her present owners in 1941 via A.R. Adams & Son whose yard was nearby.

GKN No. 17, a 1937-built Hunslet 0-6-0 saddle tank, shunts at the south end of East Moors Steelworks, Cardiff on 17 February 1962. This class was the precursor of the larger so-called 'Austerity' tanks, many of which were to be found in locations across south Wales.

Dorothy, here quietly rusting away at Pontardawe Steelworks in July 1962, was built by the Brush Electrical Engineering Co., Loughborough, in 1903 for Powesland & Mason, dock contractors for the Swansea Harbour Trust. Acquired by the GWR in 1924 and numbered 795, it was sold in 1929 to the steelworks. It was given the name it carries in the photograph when the works was acquired by Richard Thomas and Baldwins in 1947. It was condemned in 1962.

A general view of the running shed at Pontardawe Steelworks. Alongside the water tank is an unusual Beyer-Peacock 0-4-0 saddle tank of 1932. A standard Andrew Barclay product is in front of the shed. July 1962

At Pontarddulais, on the Graig Merthyr colliery system, a Barclay 0-4-0 ST of 1906 has left the rails during shunting operations. Jacks are in position and the locomotive was soon back in action. March 1963

Three years later sister engine *Glan Dulais*, showing evidence of ill-treatment, heads the colliers' one-coach train down from the pit head. 23 July 1966

In apparently totally rural surroundings alongside the river Taff, NCB No.6, a Peckett of 1945, hauls empty wagons from the exchange sidings with BR at Merthyr Vale colliery. The Taff Vale main line is in the foreground whilst, running across the top of the picture, is the alignment of the joint GWR/RR line from Quakers Yard to Merthyr, closed in 1951. 27 May 1966

Surprisingly close to the previous location, No. 6 takes a breather in a more characteristic environment. Some of the houses of Aberfan are visible in the background. 27 May 1966

Maerdy colliery, at the head of the Rhondda Fach valley, on a bright day in March 1967. Two locomotives were in steam: ex-GWR pannier tank 9792 and a 1954-built Peckett saddle tank.

Alan confesses: 'Wandering unchallenged inside the melting shop at Llanelli Steelworks and within a few feet of a pool of molten slag, without a locomotive in sight, I could not resist taking a photograph of the furnace charging machine'. 10 June 1967

One of the purpose-built, low-height Andrew Barclay locomotives of 1948 takes water outside the melting shop at Llanelli Steelworks. July 1966

Deep inside the loading area at Dyffryn Rhondda colliery, *Olga*, a 1909 Barclay goes about her business on 21 March 1967.

Against a background of typical valleys terraced houses, an Andrew Barclay 0-6-0ST crosses the river Cynon which runs through the colliery at Mountain Ash. 1968

Under the 'Big Arch' at Talywain, in the Llwyd valley between Blaenavon and Pontypool, yet another Barclay locomotive (*Islwyn* of 1952) passes the photographer's motor cycle with a permanent way train. 1 April 1967

From Talywain a colliery line led up the valley to the pit at Blaenserchan. Heading a loaded train down the valley is ex-GWR pannier tank 7754. October 1969

Patricia, a Hunslet-built Austerity 0-6-0 saddle tank of 1943, drifts past a line of loaded wagons at Caerau colliery, Maesteg. 21 March 1967

Inside the NCB running shed at Maesteg, *Norma*, nine years younger than her sister *Patricia*, prepares to leave for duty with cylinder drain cocks open. 21 March 1967

An Austerity saddle tank climbs towards St John's colliery, Maesteg. 1969

Chapter 6

DECLINE

In this section are included some images of the decline, closure and destruction of the railway.

Sometimes morbid, at others gaunt, even horrific, sometimes just desperately sad, they demonstrate Alan Jarvis's role as a photographer who likes railway subjects rather than a railway enthusiast who takes photographs. As with the best railway artists, it is the picture which is more important than the subject. Some of these images are simply unemotionally good photographic studies of odd and contorted shapes, some are oddities, some are powerful statements; at least one has a surrealist feel to it. They all serve to challenge the viewer to consider what it is about railways which so many find appealing. This book might lead some to feel that the answer lies simply in the provision of rich material for the imaginative photographic artist.

At Builth Road Low Level station in June 1964 the signal-box lever frame is exposed to the elements as the building is demolished around it. June 1964

London Underground coaches await the torch in Bird's scrapyard at Morriston, Swansea, in April 1961. They had been hauled down from London as freight trains, topped-and-tailed by brake vans specially fitted with coupling and buffing gear to match the non-standard equipment on the coaches.

At the same location in September 1962, a number of ex-Metropolitan Railway coaches had arrived for similar treatment. Some still carried destination boards to exotic places like Baker Street, Rickmansworth and Amersham.

This breakdown van, photographed at Cardiff East Dock shed yard in April 1965, was converted from a 1902 suburban brake third coach in 1937. Bearing the ominous legend 'COND', it was destined to end its days in Woodham's yard where it was dismembered in November 1965. During its time as a breakdown van it was allocated first to Didcot and later to St Blazey. April 1965.

These two vans were photographed at Canton Depot in January 1963. Marked 'For Use At Llanfyllin Only' and '. . . Shrewsbury Abbey Depot Only' they would have been parked in a siding at these places to afford temporary covered storage accommodation.

Unlike Messrs Woodham Brothers Ltd at Barry, who allowed scrapped locomotives to accumulate, other scrap dealers in south Wales, the Midlands and the north of England usually lit their acetylene torches within days of the arrival of withdrawn locomotives. This was the nightmarish scene at Cashmore's yard at Newport in June 1967. Over 200 steam locomotives have survived such a fate simply due to the good fortune of being sold to Dai Woodham, such is the haphazard nature of railway preservation.

One of the more outlandish scenes photographed at Swansea East Dock shed was this pair of Southern Region Bulleid 0-6-0s Nos. 33022 and 33010 of 1942 vintage on their sad, final journey to meet a Welsh cutting torch. 26 July 1964

Bilingual notices were more common in mid- and north Wales and not used by all companies. This Brecon and Merthyr Railway example was photographed near Rhiwderin in 1962.

Even in the mid-1960s there was still a considerable amount of original small railway 'furniture' surviving – trespass notices, station lamps, boundary posts and the like – which bore the name or initials of the pre-1923 grouping railway companies, and making a photographic record of these was another pleasant pursuit for a minority group of railway enthusiasts. In some cases they belonged to companies which had been absorbed long before the grouping. One of Alan's friends appropriately called these items 'bric-à-brac', although all such items now command far more than bric-à-brac prices on the flourishing 'railwayana' collectors' market.

Most railways marked out their ownership of land with boundary marker posts. This long-lived survivor, near Groeswen, carries the initials of the Pontypridd, Caerphilly and Newport Railway Company. Incorporated in 1878, the company was absorbed in 1897 by the Alexandra (Newport & South Wales) Dock and Railway Company. An earlier railway with the same initials (the Pontypool, Caerleon & Newport Railway) was incorporated in 1865 and absorbed by the GWR in 1876. 15 March 1964

Still supporting the platform awning at Sully when photographed in September 1960, this bracket bears the initials of the Cardiff, Penarth and Barry Junction Railway incorporated in 1885 and absorbed by the Taff Vale Railway in 1889.

Rather more difficult to decipher are the initials RSBR – Rhondda & Swansea Bay Railway
– on a similar support photographed at Aberavon Town station. 20 July 1964

The pattern-maker who set up the mould for this casting was not responsible for the
incorrect spelling of Gwendraeth. The name 'Gwendreath' is correctly quoted from the Act
of 1866 under which the company was incorporated by the amalgamation of two earlier
companies.

Chapter 7

REVIVAL

Regular steam haulage on British Railways ended in August 1968 and thirteen months later a total ban was imposed on preserved steam locomotive operation on BR tracks. This ban was lifted in October 1971 and steam made its reappearance, at first mainly in the form of locomotives which had been privately purchased from BR in working order. As the preservation movement gained momentum, more and more locomotives took the stage, the majority having been rescued from Woodham's. Three of the five preserved British locomotives featured below owe their continued existence to Dai Woodham. Of the exceptions, *City of Truro* was selected for preservation over 70 years ago and *King George V* was purchased privately from British Railways in 1968.

Steam haulage can still be seen on the main line nearly every weekend of the year. It also flourishes on many preserved lines. Sadly, in both cases, invariably in the presence of high-visibility jackets and rather too many other photographers and film makers.

But it has to be remembered that today, unlike the heady days of the 1950s and early '60s, if anything goes wrong at the last moment – such as the light changing abruptly, the camera not being ready, another train obscuring one's view – it is not possible to say, 'never mind, there'll be another one along in a few minutes'.

The first locomotive to enjoy the lifting of the ban was *King George V*. Seen here near Nantyderry, on the final leg of a 'Return to Steam' special, it looked and sounded in fine fettle as it tackled the bank on its way home to Bulmer's Cider factory at Hereford on 7 October 1971.

Ex-GWR 4-6-0 No. 5029 *Nunney Castle* and an ex-BR Standard Class 2-6-4T accelerate their special train past East Usk Junction, Newport. No. 5029 was rescued from Woodham's Barry yard after rusting away there for 12 years. Built in May 1934 and withdrawn in December 1963, it arrived at Barry in May 1964 and left for a new life at the Great Western Society's Didcot Railway Centre in May 1976. 4 April 1994

Ex-GWR 4-6-0 No. 6024 *King Edward I* rushes towards the site of the former station at Peterston-super-Ely, to the west of Cardiff, *en route* to Swansea on 20 May 1994. The sound of the exhaust had been heard for well over one minute before it appeared, leaning into the curve. The maximum speed for steam specials at the time was 60 mph and His Majesty was doing at least this as he passed. This locomotive had spent a little over 10 years at Woodham's yard.

1991 was the 150th anniversary of the completion of the Taff Vale Railway from Cardiff to Merthyr Tydfil and the event was celebrated with a number of steam specials along the lines of that company and those of the Rhymney Railway. Ex-BR Standard 2-6-4T No. 80080 makes a vociferous ascent of the 1 in 40 incline north of Abercynon on its way to Merthyr Tydfil in October 1991. No. 80080 had also escaped from Barry, after nearly 15 years.

In 1989 the 150th anniversary of the Netherlands State Railways (Nederlandische Spoorwegen) was celebrated with a week of locomotive cavalcades at Utrecht, where the National Railway Museum is located. Steam locomotives from Britain, France, Belgium, Germany (East and West), Switzerland, Austria, Czechoslovakia and Poland were present, most having reached Utrecht from distant home countries under their own steam. Britain was represented by ex-GWR 4-4-0

City of Truro of 1903, generally recognised as having exceeded 100 mph during a mail train run from Plymouth to Paddington in the following year. This performance secured the locomotive its subsequent preservation in 1931. It is seen here dwarfed by an Austrian (ex-German) 2-10-0 Class 52, a 'Kriegslok' (war locomotive). Some of the visiting locomotives hauled special trains on various routes in Holland during the festivities. *City of Truro* was unable to participate as it was not fitted with air-brake equipment, but it did take part in the twice-daily cavalcades.

The Netherlands' own principal performer was 4-6-0 express passenger locomotive No. 3737, seen here on one of its many outings during the week. This locomotive owes its survival to the fact that in 1958 it was rostered to work the last scheduled steam-hauled train in Holland and was then transferred to the museum for preservation. No. 3737 was built locally in 1911 to a design of Beyer, Peacock of Manchester. *City of Truro* would have noted with satisfaction that it sported two Swindon characteristics, a copper-capped chimney and a polished safety-valve cover and wore a livery quite close to GWR Brunswick green.

Alan concludes the chapter: 'In my opening remarks I mentioned that I did not start 35mm colour photography until 1959, having previously used monochrome 120-size roll film. Towards the end of the enjoyable task of selecting negatives for this book I happened across some roll film colour negatives, long forgotten, dating back to about 1956. I recalled that I was quite disappointed with the prints obtained at the time but now wondered whether anything better could be made of them in these days of domestic digital scanning and enhancement. Using home computer, scanning and printing equipment I have been able to inject some life and colour into these old negatives, three of which are reproduced here. Although I no longer have the original prints, I believe that these digital prints are at least as good as the originals, given that the negatives are quite grainy and may have suffered from fading over the past 45 years.

An unidentified 'Castle' Class locomotive heads past the hand-operated gates of St George's Crossing, west of Cardiff, with a Paddington to Swansea train. The three-character headcode on the smokebox door, together with the headlamps at each end of the buffer beam, denote an express passenger (Class 1) train and identify this working as 1F41 for control purposes. Reference to the working timetables of the period revealed that the train was the 12.55pm (summer Saturdays only) from Paddington to Swansea. *c*.1956

Probably taken on the same day, train 1F54 is crossing one of the many bridges over the river Ely to the west of Cardiff. Hauled by a BR Standard Class 7 4-6-2, the 3.35pm from Paddington to Fishguard Harbour has just passed through St Fagans station. *c.*1956

In the shed yard at Radyr ex-GWR 0-4-2T No. 1447 awaits minor attention. *c.*1956

'Some of the black-and-white prints in this book are also reproduced from digital prints from scanned negatives where the original negative had been over-exposed or over-developed to an extent that could not be easily corrected by adjustments at the 'wet' printing stage.

'I have been using a digital camera for several years, and although its specification is now far below that of current models, prints up to 7" x 5" are perfectly acceptable. Digital colour transparencies in the format of colour film slides are unlikely to appear. The route to the projection on a screen of images from digital cameras is already available by means of digital projectors but not yet at an affordable price for most amateur users. At the moment, a replacement bulb for these projectors costs considerably more than a well-specified slide projector.

'The three following illustrations are taken from home-produced prints from photographs taken with the digital camera.'

One of the visual advantages of privatisation of our railway system was the gradual disappearance of the universal grey-painted diesel locomotive in favour of green, blue, red and even a garish purple and white. In this view, taken from the famous Canton footbridge, the new and fast confronts the old and slow as a Class 08 0-6-0 diesel electric shunter trundles pass a brand new, 125 mph Class 67 locomotive in the shed yard. It had arrived at Newport Docks from the General Motors factory in Spain a few days before this photograph was taken in October 1999.

No less than 250 Class 66 locomotives were ordered by EWS from the GM factory at London, Ontario. Again seen from the Canton footbridge, No. 66116 heads eastwards towards Cardiff Central with a train of tank wagons. The High Speed Train is laying over in readiness for its next trip to Paddington. June 2000

Alan thought it fitting to conclude with a digital photograph of a surviving railway relic of 200 years ago. Traces of the Penydarren tramroad (opened in 1802), and on which the world's first steam railway engine ran in 1804, can still be found along the Taff valley north of Abercynon. The southern portal of the tunnel near Pentrebach has been restored for preservation as one of the earliest railway relics. June 2001

The number was familiar but little else. The photographer was pictured at the controls of the South African Railways' version of *Caerphilly Castle* in the shed yard at Mossel Bay in November 1979. No. 4073 was a member of the 'GMAM' Class of 4-8-2 + 2-8-4 Garratt locomotives of which 120 examples were built between 1952 and 1954 by the Henschel, Beyer Peacock and North British Locomotive companies.